2BROADS ABROAD
MOMS FLY THE COOP

DEBORAH SERRA   **NANCY SERRA GREENE**

PRINTED IN THE UNITED STATES OF AMERICA

Published by:
Library Tales Publishing, Inc.
511 6th Avenue #56
New York, NY 10011
www.LibraryTalesPublishing.com

For general information on our other products and services, please contact our Customer Care Department at 1-800-754-5016, or fax 917-463-0892. For technical support, please visit www.LibraryTalesPublishing.com

Library Tales Publishing also publishes its books in a variety of electronic formats. Every content that appears in print is available in electronic books.

ISBN-13: 978-0692509487
ISBN-10: 0692509488

RUNNING AWAY FROM HOME

"Your youngest is leaving for college? Aw, empty nest?" Then, sappy eyes followed by a plaintive grin and, "What *will* you do?"

Before my sister and I decided to run away from home we were bothered by that question. There was something minimizing about it, minimizing and not completely untrue. Motherhood had been so deceptive, the greatest paradox in life: every single bleary-eyed day felt a month long, and the years went by in an instant. They flashed by like lightning and left a desiccated scorch mark wearing my clothes. It was disagreeable to imagine what life would be like childless: there would be the family tree, and there would be the mom who's the center of the family tree, standing leafless, bare (and it has been a while since I looked good bare). There was some solace as I glanced around me to see my younger sister, Nancy, would be standing there bare as well. We were embarking on this progeny-shedding calamity simultaneously as both of our youngest daughters, Nicole and Olivia, were leaving for college the same week.

I knew that Nancy hadn't really focused on it yet. And then, we met at Fashion Island in Newport Beach near her home to get a birthday gift for our mom. We ran into two of Nancy's neighbors, Vicki and Susan.

"Nancy," Vicki asked, "doesn't Nicole graduate from Corona Del Mar High School this June?"

"Yes," Nancy said. "She's going to the University of Washington."

"Oh," Susan lifted her eyebrows, "you must be devastated."

"What?" Nancy looked confused. "No, actually I was happy for her. She worked really hard. It was her first choice school."

"But *so* far away!" Susan added in that annoying singsong tone.

Nancy shifted her feet, a move I knew well as her sister. It was something she always did when she was being told something she did not like to hear.

"It's not *that* far." Nancy said.

"It's a plane ride. You need an *airplane* to see your daughter." Susan said loudly.

"Yeah." Nancy turned to me in an effort to change the subject. "You remember my sister, Deborah?"

"Of course." Vicki smiled. And we exchanged hellos. Vicki seemed normal, but I had an inkling that I might have to slap Susan.

Susan continued on with her one thought. "With your son gone already, and soon Nicole, well, Nancy, I guess you're all alone now."

Nancy shifted her feet again. "I'm still married, Susan."

"Sure. Sure. Right. So that's better than nothing, huh?"

Nancy and I both froze. Did she just say that?

"You know," Vicki tried to cut off Susan, "when Terrie's youngest left she bought a Chihuahua puppy. Cutest thing you've ever seen. And the Walkers gave a room to an exchange student from Sweden," she explained happily.

Nancy nodded. "That sounds like a good plan."

Susan opened her mouth to speak again and I wasn't sure whether I should just smack her now and be done with it, or let her continue. I made the wrong choice.

"Remember Pam Winthrop?" Susan leaned in. "When her son left she started eating a pint of Ben & Jerry's every day until she put on 60 pounds. Sad, really, tragic. Even her kneecaps were fat." Then Susan turned to me, "So, Deborah, isn't your youngest graduating, too?"

"I'm leaving the country," I said.

Susan cocked her head. "What?"

"I'm leaving the country," I repeated matter-of-factly.

"So am I," Nancy said. I looked at her. I saw the decision in her eyes. "I'm going with Deborah. We're taking a long trip together – a sisters trip."

"You are?" Susan sounded a little thwarted, which Nancy found gratifying.

"Yup, in the planning stages." Nancy smiled at Susan who was clearly disappointed that we were not miserable as anticipated. "Nice to see you though, Susan, Vicki. Got to go. In the middle of booking flights and stuff. So much to do!"

We turned away and strode with purpose toward the door.

I whispered, "Susan's a real gem."

"She did me a favor."

"Yeah?"

"I've been so busy I just wasn't thinking about it."

"And I haven't been able to think about anything else," I said. "When I'm awake in the middle of the night it runs over and over in my mind."

Nancy said, "When I heard that crap Susan was dealing, all of a sudden I realized, there's no way am I plodding into that sunset with fat kneecaps carrying a Chihuahua."

"I'm with you. And by the way, that sunset? It's not like previous generations. When motherhood ends now there's a whole lot of life left. We're healthy and active, with luck we've got a good thirty years on our hands."

"We need a plan."

"We need a drink and a plan."

"A drink? Deborah, it's the middle of the afternoon."

"Let go of the rules, Nance. Just let go."

This was one of our fundamental differences. Nancy appreciated rules. They worked with her planning brain and her organized life. I've always felt offended by rules. Rules made me irritable.

We took a left turn and grabbed some seats in the bar area of a little restaurant across the street. I ordered two cold tequila shots and we looked ahead together. With our girls scheduled to leave home shortly our everyday lives were about to evaporate.

"Nancy, we have to do something. Looking ahead, all I see is…waiting."

"Waiting?" Nancy asked.

"Waiting for school breaks, waiting for our husbands to come home from work, waiting for the holidays, waiting for the kids to call, waiting to say hello and then goodbye again, and then to continue waiting…"

"God, that sucks." Nancy raised her tequila shot glass. "No waiting."

"No waiting."

And we threw back the tequila. We were on the same page.

Waiting hurts. It not only hurts because waiting for the people you love always hurts, but also because we didn't like who that made us: we are energetic women not inclined to waiting. I had always worked as a writer during the hours that my kids were in school, and Nancy, well, she simply ran everything. As soon as others found out how organized and competent she was they asked her to take officer positions on the PTA, the Assistance League, and the School Fundraiser. She published the neighborhood newsletter; she was Sports Team Mom, Classroom Mom, Field Trip Mom, and it went on and on. Nancy accomplished more in one day than most women do in a month. We had been frenetic with kids, and house upkeep, and budgets, and activities, but now, we passed the tequila bottle and considered our options. We would need to handle the emotional loss and also kick-start our lives in a completely different direction. We needed an adventure, and based on the depth of the despondency, probably more than one — perhaps a series of adventures.

Personally, I was feeling pretty burned the day I realized that motherhood was a temp job, with spectacular benefits, but rather limited as a reference for a "real" job. You know, in the real world where professional women wear dark expensive beautifully tailored suits, engage in intelligent repartee, have short spunky hair, and don't know what being Snack Mom means. And while there were plenty of days I longed for the adult conversation and intellectual connection of the corporate world, it wasn't the choice either of us made. Nancy and I were both aware and grateful to even have a choice. And we did know these moments of lifestyle envy went both ways. All choices have their sacrifices, but the corporate choice does not have this sudden and absolute cessation of responsibility, unless you've been fired, which I have been, and FYI that doesn't feel good either.

We've seen a plethora of magazines and researchers

devoting time and money to post-partum depression, well, welcome to post-parental depression, which without intervention may actually last for the rest of your livelong days. I looked around and wondered, what were the options? Whatever the reason your last kid moves out, whether it's college, or a new job, a marriage, the military, or a desire to live out of his or her car, regardless, it is the final change in the daily life of a career mom. (We prefer career mom since stay-at-home-mom makes us feel like we're under house arrest.) The prospect of this transition banged around in my mind for months as it got closer and closer. I was relieved that I could share it with my sister now.

While there was no discounting the loss we were feeling and the raw sensitivity that overwhelms when a child moves on, we knew that what we had to do was to turn "lonely" into "free". We were going to be free for the first time in 20 years, free to arrange our time. On the one hand, we had no children to anchor our days — on the other hand, we had no anchor. We could drift or we could set a course. The very thing that felt unnerving about losing the structure of our days was giving us access to choices we'd not had before. There was no one to attend to, no children stopping us from taking off and going somewhere; maybe what we really needed to do was get the hell out of Dodge.

Travel? Why not? There were so many places Nancy and I had never seen: the Badlands of South Dakota, the Grand Canyon, the Smokey Mountains, not to mention Vienna or Sydney. We could plan a trip and perhaps rediscover the two little girls we once were together. Putting some distance between us and our family home after we dropped off our girls seemed like a sound idea.

The looming exodus barreled down on us and picked up speed in August. All the typical activities took on an added dimension. The house was filled with the usual loud, sloppy teenagers enjoying the last gasp of summer break. We observed it all to the sound of a ticking clock. Soon no neighborhood teenage boys were going to throw open our front door and walk directly to our refrigerator like it was their own. No little girls were to be found with tiny bottles of glittery blue nail polish working on their toenails while perched precariously on our most fragile piece of furniture. No arguing would be heard between siblings. No glasses stacked on top of nightstands. No half-eaten remnants of cheap Mexican food wrapped in mysterious foil and becoming fungus colonies in the pantry. No tire marks to be seen over the grass where the driveway had been misjudged. No doors left open with the heat on. No more lengthy explanations on how washing the countertop is actually part of doing the dishes. No boxes of cereal with four flakes in them. No curious profusion of ping-pong balls even though we do not have a ping-pong table. No washing machine wars. And also, no moments of sudden laughter, no dance programs, or volleyball games, no moments of peeking in while they're sleeping, no moments of *unplanned* togetherness. I suppose that's the worst of it – the fact that now we must *plan* to be together. Yes, that's the worst, that being with each other is no longer the default.

For the past 20 years, every morning, afternoon, and night, like all moms we put everyone else's needs before our own: children, husband, home, friends, neighbors, hamsters. We did it because we cared to, no one demanded it, and there was a lot to feel good about, and memories too precious to replace. We have no regrets. Our husbands watched us do this day-in and day-out for over two decades, and they understood that along with all the joy of that comes the feeling of being support staff in someone else's life instead of wholly in one's own life. (Okay, maybe they didn't understand it, maybe we had to explain to them regularly, but they got it.) We thought about how to approach Nancy's husband, Chip, and my husband, Larry, about our decision to take a trip. We hadn't traveled without our husbands in over 20 years.

"Deborah," Nancy cautioned me, "I think it's going to be hard for them, too, when the girls leave. They've been good dads and they are also losing, not just us."

"But it's different. They have outside-the-home jobs and whole other lives that aren't changing at all; their every day remains the same."

"True." Nancy cautioned me. "But I don't think we should assume they aren't emotional about it, too."

"Yeah, that's true. I'll be diplomatic. I'll bring up the idea and then gently convince them how right it is for you and me to take this trip together."

"Deborah, just don't be too blunt. You have a tendency to get impatient and be blunt."

"No, I don't."

"Yes, you do."

"I won't be blunt."

"Or impatient."

"Or impatient."

"I don't want them to feel like they're being left behind, too," Nancy said.

"Okay, I'll be subtle."

"Can you do subtle?"

"Subtle is my middle name."

"Anne is your middle name."

"Sisters really do know everything."

Nancy and Chip drove the hour to our home for dinner. Once we had started eating Nancy broached the topic. "Our girls will be moving away pretty soon."

My husband, Larry, said, "All those years when they're growing and random people keep telling you that it goes by so fast and you're still surprised when it does."

Chip said, "Right, although, think how everything will be easier from now on. More kicking back with the guys or..."

"Or travel." I added cheerfully.

"They've opened a bunch of micro breweries in San Diego. Maybe we should go one Saturday and check them out?" Larry said.

"Yeah!" Chip said. "If it's downtown we could bike from one to the other and make a day of it."

"Great idea," Larry said, "and how about no more tip-toeing around the house on weekend mornings until noon. Teenagers log more time in the sack than hibernating bears."

"And travel sounds like a terrific option," I added. "Nancy and I were thinking..."

"Could you believe that?" Chip interrupted agreeing vehemently with Larry. "Drove me crazy when they slept until noon. I don't remember ever doing that. I used to pace outside of their bedroom door making coughing sounds it annoyed me so much."

Larry said, "I'm looking forward to just chilling here in the quiet and enjoying our home."

Chip added with a huge grin, "And a full refrigerator."

"But an empty quiet home," I said and looked at Nancy. They didn't seem quite as emotional over this transition as we were. Nancy shrugged slightly and smiled at me.

"Exactly," Larry said. "No video games blaring."

"And," Chip raised his fork to make the point, "no reality TV shows, or nights when we have to stay up forever because..."

I blurted out, "Nancy and I are running away from home."

Both men looked at me.

"We're leaving the country."

Nancy raised her eyebrows and spoke with a questioning tone, "Really, Deborah? Subtle is your middle name?"

"They're talking about how great it's going it be."

She turned to the guys and explained. "We've decided to take a trip together, a sister trip, get away from home, to jump-start this new phase of our lives. It'll be a lot cheaper since we'll be splitting all the costs and we can use points from our credit card to get an airline ticket."

Both our guys looked a little shell-shocked, but they also knew we were on short emotional leashes. Neither one of them wanted to speak first so I kept going.

"And if it goes well we're thinking maybe we'll take a couple of trips over the next several years." I added, "2 Broads Abroad!"

There was a long hesitation as they let it settle in and weighed out the correct response.

Cautiously, testing the water, Larry said, "Um... great?"

Chip agreed. "So...that would mean...Larry and I will be here on our own?"

"Exactly," I said. "Bike ride to every brewery on the west coast if you want."

You know how when you're married to someone there are those moments when you know to back off even though you may not understand why or agree? It is a sixth sense that comes from living with someone for so many years. This was one of those times and both our guys recognized it. They forced smiles, exchanged a look, and went back to eating. It was settled.

THE COLLEGE GIRLS PACK-UP

Clothing was layered into colored heaps all over the carpeted floor in my daughter's bedroom as she struggled to make choices about what to bring to college. Her concept was everything must go, and our concept was only two extra baggage charges. So we negotiated. I kept my voice light, and a grin on my face the entire time, as she flung shirts out of her closet. Occasionally, a particular addition to the pile might force a comment.

"But, honey, that's a costume."

"Mom, what if I need this leopard print, furry armed, stretchy, one-piece suit thing?"

"You mean, like if there's a contest for Most Ridiculous Outfit?"

"You don't know. You don't know if I might need it."

"I believe to a moral certainty you will not need that."

"Will you send it to me if I need it?"

"Ah, sure I will." And I knew I would not and that this crazy clinging behavior was to be expected. I'd seen it with her sister. They felt better to be prepared to the point of absurdity. It was not the case for their brother, who was certain he was forgetting things and figured as long as he had a pair of gym shorts, his electronics, and his stock portfolio (yes, at 18) everything else was fungible.

When Olivia ran down to the garage to collect her boots to pack, I had a moment alone in her bedroom. Sitting cross-legged on the floor, I exchanged knowing nods with her stuffed animals. They weren't going either, and those inanimate critters had never looked more alive to me. My eyes sought out that one special animal; the one she slept with every night, a large stuffed pink pig that we'd convinced her was there to protect her. It was Protecto-Piggy, we had told her as we desperately hoped she would stop waking us up in the middle of the night. Then, when she became a teenager, we lay awake late at night worrying about other possibilities. I supposed I should focus on all the great sleep I was going to get now.

Nancy, who understood better than I did why a girl leaving for college would need every single thing in her closest, didn't fight it. They loaded-up a couple of duffle bags full of clothes and then began packing-up the rest in boxes that were going UPS. She thought there was a very good possibility there would be a Most Ridiculous Outfit contest and her daughter would be prepared. This actually gave Nancy a stab in the heart a few days after Nicole left when she walked into her daughter's bedroom, where the closet door was left open, and there were only hangers. A row of naked, lonely, useless hangers — an actual visual representation of how she felt: empty, hanging. Nancy forgot where she'd been headed and sat down on Nicole's bed noticing how perfectly made it was. Then, stillness. No one was home. She sat there for a long time. Her eyes moved slowly around the bedroom and she saw the pens on the desk were actually in the pen jar, and the books on the shelf were all neatly lined up. She let herself remember for a moment that book her daughter made in grade school about her favorite animal and she found it there on the shelf – also left behind. She could see that every single thing in the room was in its proper place and thought, "Doesn't everything look so perfect for being so completely wrong." And she lost it.

In actuality, there is a one particular moment when a mother faces that her child is leaving. It is not as if we didn't always know it, but the chores of being a mother are relentless, so we didn't really feel what was coming until it hit us in the face.

For me, that moment was the day my youngest child got her driver's license. For all practical purposes, that was the moment the physical demands of motherhood came to an abrupt end. I handed her the car keys with a mixture of pride and trepidation and watched as she gleefully laid rubber out of our driveway. I was no longer needed in that most essential way: on a metaphorical and a practical level she could get where she was going without me. Standing in the doorway, I felt like Alice in Wonderland as the world around me stretched, and I wondered when did this house get so spacious, and so still?

For Nancy, that sudden moment came in a letter. Ripping open bills at the kitchen table while answering the phone *and* chopping onions she opened and found the college acceptance letter for her son. "Congratulations," it said cheerfully. She put down the knife, hung up the phone, and grabbed the Chardonnay. Sure, it was what they'd been working towards, what they'd been waiting for; it fulfilled their hopes for her son's future. It was everything they wanted, but in that moment, alone at the kitchen table, which is the very heart of a family, she knew her family would never be quite the same. He was leaving and it all felt painfully sudden. A moment later, when her son and his best friend clomped into the kitchen heading for the chips and salsa, he suddenly looked to her like a kid who had never done a single wrong thing (this was when she should've put down the bottle). Yes, he was absolutely perfect, the perfect son, the perfect older brother. He'd always been the perfect son. Her eyes welled...seriously, put down the bottle.

As those last few months progressed, our two youngest were less and less frequently at home as they frolicked through their senior year. The demands on our time were falling away. For moms, relegated to the do-you-need-food-or-water pay grade in our kids' eyes, it seemed that even our homes were callously turning against us. That was when I started hearing things.

"Larry?" I whispered from my cell phone as I stood behind our bedroom door.

"Yeah, what's wrong? Why are you whispering?"

"There's someone in the house."

"What?"

"I hear someone downstairs."

"Get out. I'll call 9-1-1."

"No, it might be nothing. I want to check. But I want you on the phone while I do in case."

"Have you lost your mind? I'm calling 9-1-1."

"Okay, here I go, downstairs. It's probably nothing but..."

"Deborah, please..."

"No one in the kitchen."

"Go outside now!"

"No one in the family room. Hmmm...okay, I checked, oh, guess it's nothing."

"Nothing? Don't search any further, because I'm going to kill you myself when I get home."

"Sorry, honey." I hung up, but I sill heard things.

What *was* all that noise? Noises I'd never heard be-fore, because I didn't know that empty actually made noise. The house groaned. The roof crackled here and there. The windows made some kind of popping sound when the sun hit the glass. Someone was humming. What on earth was all that humming? I investigated. The refrigerator? The refrigerator makes that much noise? And it wasn't only the refrigerator, it was: the light bulbs, the clocks, the cable modem, the heater, the computer, the back-up drive. I was suddenly sur-rounded by sounds I'd never noticed before – lonely hollow sounds. But it was worse for Nancy. She lived in a younger neighborhood and she sat in her family room riveted to the sounds of little kids playing out-side. Someone else's six-year-old was kicking the soccer ball and someone else's eight-year-old was riding his skateboard. It was actually painful to hear those little voices yelling and laughing and echoing inside her emp-ty house. All that happy noise made for a profoundly heavy heart.

When we thought about the phases of our lives at each juncture of change: our own departure from home, our first real job, our marriages, the birth of our chil-dren, all of the big phases of change held out something new for us. This change was shaping up very different-ly. This change was loss – complete dissolution of the fundamental family structure forever and that was all. We had to plan. We needed to be proactive. The alterna-tive was to be left standing frozen in time, in a life that had moved on without us, and to become observers and visitors in our kids' lives. Not acceptable. So, we set our imaginations loose.

We considered our location. Now that we knew we were leaving – where could we go?

"Angkor Wat," I said.

"Wat what?" Nancy asked.

"It's the largest temple in the world, built in 1125."

"Where is it?"

"Cambodia."

"Uh, huh. Deborah, I was thinking more along the lines of a bucolic vineyard in Tuscany. You know, stroll along the hills, sample the fruit of the vine, nectar of the gods?"

"Oh. Okay, how would you feel about a camel trek in Morocco?"

"Probably sore, smelly, and hot. And I understand camels are mean and they spit. They spit, Deborah. What about a civilized boat ride down the Rhine River in Germany? They have castles and I know how you like castles."

"I do like castles, but don't you think we should go more exotic?"

"This is our first trip together. I'd like to steer clear of nations at war, places we'd need to wear a burka, or can't speak the language, or ride on an angry animal. Surely we can agree on somewhere."

"I've always wanted to see where grandma's family came from."

"Me, too!"

"With a little research and a rental car we can see the entire island in a couple of weeks."

"Perfect. Ireland it is!"

As we prepared for our trip, we learned that two mid-life married sisters planning an elaborate trip over five thousand miles from home, *not* inviting their husbands, and not going for a wedding, or some other acceptable archetypal event, created a cognitive disturbance. There were critical elements to consider and that others were only too happy to point out. Were we just planning on letting the mail pile up, bowing out of our exercise routine, letting the milk sour in the fridge, letting the house run haphazardly without management, while knowing our husbands would forget to close the windows and never lock the door, and then they'll return to a vacant home and have to fend for themselves? Were we aware that if we were not around, then the house phone would ring and ring and our husbands would never answer it or check the messages, nor would they wash their sheets, towels, or anything other than their underwear, and only after they'd turned that last pair inside-out. (In reality, I learned later, my husband went to Ross For Less and bought new underwear rather than wash his.) And what if we were not reachable for the kids in that one important moment? We pondered all of these exigencies. We struggled with the maternal imperative: to be all, to do all, to fix all, and we decided – screw it, we're outta here.

This attitude was somehow suspect and seemed to provoke two reactions in those around us: either, a narrow-eyed questioning that seemed to hint at an underlying reckless selfishness, or an ecstatic longing so intense with envy it was palpable in the air. There were actually a few husbands who said aloud they'd "never let their wife do that". Let? Really? That paternalistic mindset disguised as concern was most offensive. It made us appreciate our own husbands so much more, which they saw as the one and only plus of this whole adventure. Our macho men assured us they could handle absolutely everything, no sweat, which we knew was absolutely untrue, because we were aware that they didn't even know what "everything" was. It was important, for once in our lives, to let go of the reins.

A FEW HELPFUL TIPS
FROM FRIENDS

Ireland: The Emerald Isle. We were lost in musings about the lush verdant rolling hills of Connemara, the craggy seaside western shore, the Dublin pubs, the castles, rainbows, faeries and leprechauns. What little girl hasn't dressed-up like a faerie and pretended to live in a castle, which was actually the discarded cardboard TV box in their basement? Ireland was romantic, historic, visually beautiful, and we were connected through our own mother. We could learn about the history, become expert travelers, and share it all. It was perfect. The excitement was distracting and gave us something fresh to focus on.

Then, some friends and relatives, you know, just to be helpful, brought up a few concerns, a few helpful warnings that escalated, gathered force, bordered on the hysterical, and fell headlong into the absurd. It seemed everyone had heard of some unfortunate woman who had had a grave, even life-threatening issue while traveling, and each of them felt fundamentally compelled to share these stories with us: my friend was trapped in a Dublin restroom for 13 hours; whatever you do don't be on the streets when the bars close; my mother lost her passport; my sister was pick-pocketed, and then the ATM ate her card, the hotel canceled her reservation and she had to sleep on the bus; were we prepared for the bed bugs?

We listened politely as we heard countless stories of lost people who missed their bus, their plane, their train, and who fell onto the metro tracks. (And Ireland doesn't have a metro.) One woman told me in a cryptic whisper that her aunt went to Ireland and she never heard from her again. (I knew this woman and I was not surprised her aunt split.)

Had we seriously considered the threat level? Is it orange? Are we at orange? Orange sounded serious, does anyone know what orange means? Do we still have colors? And, since we are, after all, Americans, it was suggested we practice claiming to be Canadian before we go, since no one is offended by Canadians. By the way, had we heard that every year in the famous Irish fog people walked right off the Cliffs of Moher, or got blown off by a rogue wind? And if the Cliffs of Moher didn't kill us, then the ring of spike rocks under the Iron Age Fort Dun Aengus on the Aran Islands fatally impales hapless tourists regularly.

Did we know the buses in Dublin are oddly tall and prone to topple? But as unreliable as public transit was, it was certainly better than driving. Surely we had heard that the Irish drive on the wrong side of the road? Intersections become bumper car death traps. The cars there have no automatic transmissions, so not only are you on the wrong side, you're driving with the wrong hand. Did our health insurance cover us in Ireland? Do we have a Med-Jet evacuation plan? And if we insist on driving, we must know the roads are extremely narrow, not enough for even two cars to pass safely, and the Irish drive so fast. And everyone knows there are no road signs – no good signs, whatsoever, anywhere on the island, which is why we were destined to get completely lost, in the middle of god knows where, probably after a car accident, with no cash, and no husbands.

Should we survive our road trip (very doubtful) we would surely become ill from the Irish food. The food is not reputed to be good and that is why they drink so much beer, beer that they drink right before they get back on the wrong side of the road to drive. If we contract some food borne illness or other malady we will not be able to get the same medications, so it's imperative we bring at a minimum: Immodium, Aleve, Ambein, Prilosec, Senikot, Claritin, Afrin, Neosporin, Tylenol, several Ace bandages and a neck brace.

One particular family friend felt strongly that he was the one to help us with money advice. We should make sure we have plenty of euro before we go and definitely shop for the best exchange rate. Do not use our credit cards, if we could help it, because of hidden fees. And then we heard the most outrageous suggestion of our entire trip. We should wear a money belt. Nancy looked at him as if he'd suggested we fly naked. I told him plainly that I was comfortable speaking for every woman in the world when I say that hell would freeze over before we voluntarily add four inches to our waistline. We're middle-aged – not dead – we still care.

After all of those helpful comments came the more personally targeted concerns. Had we ever traveled together before? Just the two of us? Could be trouble. Had we considered the possible lasting damage done to our relationship? Travel can be stressful: airports, time changes, long lines, delays, expenses, threats and warnings. It can be hard to travel with another person, share a room, share a car, share your meals, or share a hairbrush. I tried to ease minds – this was my little sister. Okay, she is 5'9" and I'm 5'5", and we are both in our fifties, but she is now, was then, and will always be my little sister.

I tried to explain this to my youngest daughter one day when she was in junior high school; in utter frustration, Olivia turned to me and demanded to know exactly when her older brother would stop treating her like she was little. I smiled and said with complete confidence, "Oh, honey, that will never happen. No matter how many gray hairs you grow, or children of your own you have, you will always be his little sister with all the joys and annoyances that brings. The dynamics of that relationship are immutable. There is something wonderful in that, something special, celebrate it." She wasn't in the mood for celebrating, she was in the mood for ripping his face off, but I could see the flicker of resignation. In the same way, Nancy understands that no matter how wrinkled, decrepit, dazed, or cranky we both become, she will always be my little sister. I really wasn't the least bit worried about traveling with her. Even as the warnings took on some rather disturbing content when Chip pulled me aside.

"Hey, Deborah, great trip you guys are planning. So, ah, I thought I'd better let you know, Nancy screams in the middle of the night."

"Screams?"

"I mean a blood-curdling, full-throated, let her rip, scream. She suddenly bolts up in bed and screams at the top of her lungs."

"Why?"

"Don't know."

"Every night?'

"No, but a lot of nights, and more often when she's

26

traveling."

"Oh."

"It's loud."

"What do you do?"

"For the first couple of years I jumped out of bed panicked, but we're married over 20 years now so I just shove her and tell her to go to sleep. Thought you should know, so, you know, you're not surprised."

"Kind of feel like I'm going to be surprised anyway."

"Yeah, it's pretty scary the first 300 times. But don't bring it up because it upsets her and makes it worse."

"Perfect."

"And make sure you close the closet door."

"Why?"

"Nancy wears contacts. Her eyesight sucks. When she screams she wakes herself up, and if the closet door is opened she sees the clothes hanging there, and since it's all blurry, she thinks it's a person in the room, and she just keeps screaming."

"Okay, close closet door, got it."

"And Nancy really likes a schedule: a plan, itinerary, maps, loves maps, that kind of thing."

I filed this information away and decided not to spend too much time thinking about it.

In the other room, my Larry had pulled Nancy aside.

"Ah, Nance, since you'll be traveling together I just thought you'll need to be aware that Deborah's bladder is the size of a gnat."

"I see."

"Resign yourself to visiting every single toilet in Ireland, kind of touring by the seat of your pants."

"Sounds like a cultural education."

"And she has the worst insomnia so don't be surprised if you wake up in the middle of the night to see her under the covers with a flashlight reading."

"Really?"

"I bought her these cool glasses that have little head-lights on them for reading at night in bed, but she says they're not bright enough. Also, she can't go anywhere in the a.m. without a hot cup of coffee first."

"I don't drink coffee."

"I know."

"And she gets cranky it if it takes someone longer than 15 minutes to get ready and go out."

"Fifteen minutes?"

"Exactly, including shower. And just as an aside, she's fairly hostile towards itineraries and has an angry relationship with maps, so I thought you might need a heads-up on that. Oh, and you'll have to force her to stop and take pictures."

"I'm a photographer. That's my goal."

"Right. She doesn't like to stop and take pictures of anything, but then she is happy later when she has them, so you'll need to push her on that."

"Ah, push her, got it. Should be interesting," Nancy said.

Later that evening, Larry and I settled in together on our cushy green sofa and he hit the guide button on the TV remote. And it began, 20 minutes of him pressing the remote arrows searching up-and-down-and-up-up–up-and-down. It's some kind of repetitive motion do-loop. I've learned to try and watch the little box in the upper corner of the TV because it shows something while he scans in a transfixed OCD state. He searches, reading each entry, but never clicks on anything. Every once in a while I'll erupt with "pick something – anything", but I've learned it's better to squint at the little box and wait it out until he gets sleepy. It's a mystery to me what he's looking for, but somehow it's therapeutic for him.

"Nothing on." He said.

"We have a hundred channels."

"Nothing on." And he continued down-down-down.

"So, you're getting ready for Ireland, huh?"

"Yup."

"Excited?"

"Yup."

"I guess I'm going to be all alone here, then."

"Larry, there must be things you've wanted to do, but didn't do because you didn't have the time, or because you knew I didn't want to? So, do them now — go watch basketball at the sports bar."

"Deborah, it's August."

"And?"

"Again, Deborah, sports have seasons. It's like telling me to go skiing in June."

"Oh, no basketball, then?"

"No."

"The point is be on your own schedule – take this opportunity to make it only about you: work early, or stay late, leave your stinky socks and damp gym clothes all over the floor, call Tom or Ben and go to a whatever kind of game happens in August. Go to those new breweries with Chip, and when you come back, order pizza and *eat it in bed.*"

"Now, you're scaring me. Who are you and what have you done with Deborah?" He kept pressing the remote arrows, up-up-down-up. "I'm going to miss you."

"That's not a bad thing, you know? And it *is* my turn."

"Is it?"

"When the kids were little you traveled all the time."

"For work."

"I know. But I was left behind while you were going places and I was envious. And not only was I left behind, I was left behind every night with twin two-year-olds and an infant."

"Yeah, I know that was hard."

"And then, on our 10th anniversary, when I hadn't slept in over five years because the twins were five, and Olivia was three, you bought me a *puppy*."

"Looking back, that might not have been the smartest move. But I was gone a lot and I thought you needed the company and we loved that crazy dog."

"We did. I don't know if I told you, but my mom called the night you gave me that puppy."

"She did?"

"She said she thought you were trying to kill me."

Larry laughed and kept hitting down-down-down-up.

"And now," I felt my throat closing up. "Now, the dog is long gone, our twins are gone, our littlest one is packed, and I don't want it all to be over. Part of who I am, the big part, is gone with them." He stopped pressing the remote and looked at me as I continued. "I feel weepy all the time and I know it's ridiculous because they're good kids and they're on their way, and of course, I *want* that for them...still, this sense that I've lost something precious that'll never come back, the loneliness, the quiet, it's all harder than I ever imagined."

Larry put his arm around me and said quietly, "I know it's different for you than for me. I get to work every morning and there's activity and controlled chaos – phones, meetings, all of that is the same for me. It's distracting and energizing. I'm glad you're doing this trip. And you *will* find pizza stains on the sheets when you return." Up-up-down-up-up-down-down-down.

PRE-GAME DUBLIN

To really enjoy a trip somewhere you have to do a little pre-game research. The more you know the more interesting a place becomes. So as Nancy and I scurried around buying things like those scratchy extra long twin sheet sets and shower caddies for our two girls who would be living in dorm rooms, we began reading.

Evidently, Dublin was founded circa 840 by those happy-go-lucky Vikings known for their motto: what's-mine-is-mine and what's-yours-is-mine. They used Dublin as a winter camp from whence they spread out into the Irish countryside like an ink stain on white linen. These were grown-ups who had not learned to keep their hands to themselves, and particularly liked picking on monasteries where lots of loot was stashed. Sitting at the mouth of the River Liffey, they called their village "Dubh Linn", which translates as black pool. A dark muddy pool of water, covered over in the 1800s, used to be in front of what is now the Coach House and Castle Gardens. (And by the way, the Vikings did not really wear that ridiculous horned helmet you put on your son when he played Leif Ericson in the first grade play. For that, you can thank the costume designer of a Wagnerian opera.) One of the reasons that the Vikings were so successful pillaging the Emerald Isle was because the Irish were deeply devoted to fighting each other, and so they didn't organize against the intruders, as they should have. The Vikings were quite successful at raiding and generally harassing the locals, but little by little, they settled in, they began to see the Irish lassies as rather fetching; they put down their weapons, intermarried, and the two cultures started a blended existence.

Fade in about one thousand years later and those pesky Vikings are still causing trouble in Dublin because not long ago workers discovered the original Viking settlement on Wood Quay in central Dublin. There was quite a clash between the Irish folk with an interest in preserving the site, and the Dublin Corporation's desire to place their modern high rise glass civic office building there. Seems to have been a fairly nasty throwdown. A vociferous public outcry demanded the development be stopped or redesigned to save the ancient and valuable site. Vociferous, yes, victorious, no. They lost because, really, if you've seen one ancient Viking settlement you've seen 'em all. When the high rise was completed the Dublin City Council moved right in. Their offices stand exactly over the site, with one of their responsibilities being...city planning.

Currently, Dublin is home to a wee bit over a million residents. It's a little city. Nancy and I liked the size, feeling it would be manageable. At that size, we would have a good chance of really seeing it. It was a good choice for our first stop. We studied the island and tried to determine what our path would be, and while navigating around the web we found ourselves routed several times to an historic hotel called The Shelbourne.

The Shelbourne has always been part of the glamorous heartbeat of Dublin. It was the Go To place for the famous and the infamous. There were sophisticated historical events like the signing of the country's constitution. There were the dignitaries: Indira Gandhi, John F. Kennedy, the Queen of Tonga, and Princess Grace, and then there were the other ones: James Cagney who danced on the Shelbourne piano; Alois Hitler (the brother) who was a waiter there; Peter O'Toole who took a bath in champagne and needed to have his toes tickled to get up in the morning (which one of the valets actually did). Also, Tara Browne lived there for a spell as a child. He was a great favorite of the Shelbourne staff. Tara was a member of the London Counter-culture in the 1960s, which seems odd since he was garishly wealthy and that should have made him a Fat Cat. He was the son of a longtime member of the House of Lords and the Guinness brewery heiress. At 21 years old, speeding in his Lotus Elan through the streets of London, he ran a red light, crashed, and died. Why are you interested in this kid? Because he was a friend of John Lennon's who was talking about him in the song "A Day In The Life". Perhaps the coolest obituary of all time – remember this?

> *He blew his mind out in a car*
> *He didn't notice that the lights had changed*
> *A crowd of people stood and stared*
> *They'd seen his face before*
> *Nobody was really sure*
> *If he was from the House of Lords*

It is The Horseshoe Bar in The Shelbourne that has seen the most action throughout the years. It was once said that the Horseshoe Bar was where a woman with a past met a man with no future. Nancy and I looked at the room rate online, a non-refundable rate of 220 dollars a night (110 dollars each), and we could definitely manage that if we were careful with our eating out and looked for better hotel bargains along the way. Our first two nights in Dublin, we would splurge.

HOW EMPTY IS YOUR BASKET?

I stayed away from my kids' bedroom, from all three of their bedrooms, those first couple of weeks after the last college drop-off. I threw myself into preparing with Nancy for our impending trip and I was doing okay, and then I went to the market. Going to the supermarket is a lot like driving a car: you are aware you're doing it, but it has become efficiently mechanical from years of repetition.

Blasting my way down the cereal aisle, I grabbed the Honey Nut Cheerios and screeched to a halt. Everything outside of me faded away. I stared at the box in my hand and took in a quick gulp of air.

Oh, I don't....I don't eat cereal. My husband doesn't eat cereal. Everyone I have bought cereal for is gone. My twins are gone. My little one is gone. Ouch. The harried mother behind me made a noise. I was blocking the aisle. I looked over at her with her overflowing cart and her cute kid in the seat.

I held up the cereal box trying to make her understand. "I don't need this anymore."

Agitated, she looked ahead and passed on the right.

I went back to pushing my cart – but slowly now because suddenly everything had changed. Those granola bars – don't need those. They were for my daughter. Her favorite. She's left. And so it went, down every aisle, all the way through the store. It was a poignantly painful experience: Dole juice – nope. Gogurt – nope. Both chunky and smooth peanut butter – nope. I was heartsick. I got a few anxious glances when I lost it in front of the acne wipes.

I pulled up to the check stand and looked down. My basket was nearly empty: coffee, spinach, and one can of tuna. I shifted my weight back and forth while waiting my turn in line. I tried to maintain, feeling embarrassingly silly, but abandoned to the emotion nonetheless. I glanced around for some kind of a distraction. An elderly lady, alone, waiting in line behind me, smiled. She carried one of those green hand-held baskets. I hadn't grabbed one of those in 20 years. Inside it she had put a single stick of butter and one apple. A single stick of butter and one apple. Oh. Oh, dear. I kept my face perfectly calm as tears spilled down my cheeks and my throat clamped shut.

The cashier looked up and asked me merrily, "Did you find everything you need?"

I looked at her, "No, I lost everything I need."

I started considering ways to avoid the market and fell into a full-scale boycott. A few days after that humiliating emotional whiplash, I pulled up in front of the supermarket and asked Larry if he would please run in and grab a carton of orange juice. I'd circle the lot. It was raining, and being a chivalrous kind of guy, he leapt out of the car and dashed into the store.

I figured – orange juice should take four minutes max: grab the carton, quick dart to the self-check, whip through the bar code, pay, and blast out the door. No brainer. I waited in the car.

Ask any woman trailing a kid or two where any item is in a store of 20,000 items and she can tell you: two aisles down, middle row, left side, under the croutons. It may not be a sexy or impressive skill, but it is nevertheless an acquired skill. When women give birth their brain becomes a scanning device capable of seeing many things at once. This is an adaptive and important ability. The old aphorism is true: women are gatherers; men are hunters. While Mom can fry chicken, help one child with homework, follow along as another practices the piano, dispute a credit card charge over the phone, and stretch-out her hamstrings all at the same time — Dad will bark "Don't talk to me, I'm on the phone." Single focus versus multi-focus capabilities. It is this ability to scan an environment as a whole that makes it easy for a woman to know where things are, and why women often hear "Have you seen my..." followed by a litany of everything in existence: car keys, wallets, homework, school ID, retainers, dental floss, Mother's Day gift, etc. So the supermarket was a breeze. I buzzed up and down the aisles with the cart, never coming to a complete stop, buying the usual items and filling it to the brim, moving efficiently while simultaneously composing in my head the email I needed to write supporting my third grader, Anna, who had refused to participate in the science experiment which was "mean to the mouse" and had rallied seven other students to follow her out of the classroom.

Now, waiting in the car for my husband, outside the supermarket the minutes ticked by. Then, I was forced to engage in the familiar circle pattern around the parking aisles, each time, scanning for him. I could have squeezed the oranges myself by now. Eventually I came to the conclusion that there must have been some kind of accident. Maybe my husband slipped and knocked over a display of salad dressing, or he was hit by some kind of falling debris. Maybe he's lying on the floor unconscious at that very moment. I started scanning for emergency vehicles. And then, he emerged through the automatic doors and there he was, 12 minutes later with the one item – one.

"What happened?' I asked flabbergasted and he climbed back into the car.

"What? Here it is." The victorious grin.

"Why did it take so long?"

"It didn't."

"Twelve minutes to get one carton of orange juice?"

"I had to find the juice."

"The refrigerated section? You know, big refrigerators."

"And then there were a lot of choices."

"You *only* like one kind."

"Yeah, that's what I got."

"Okay, good." I knew my boycott of the supermarket would have to end.

THE PLANNING STAGE

As Nancy and I attended to the final decisions of our trip we bumped into Nancy's neighbor Susan again. Evidently, Vicki had had enough since Susan was out trolling unsuspecting neighbors on her own.

"You realize that they have no Americans With Disabilities Act in the UK," Susan said as she leaned in toward me.

Susan stood too close and never blinked. Have you ever tried to have a reasonable conversation with someone who doesn't blink? You look at one eye, then become uncomfortable and look at the other eye, then you think, "Maybe I'll look down." I spent more time strategizing about where to put my gaze than listening to her babble. Susan was nosy and toxic, not that I'm judging or anything. I exchanged a look with Nancy who raised her eyebrows at me as a warning. I knew she was concerned about what I might say because she thinks that sometimes I'm blunt or impatient, which is absolutely untrue, or at least only modestly true. Gossipy negative women are a flash point for me. (Nancy claims I have several flash points, but...naw...what do little sisters know anyway?)

Trying very hard to keep the scorn out of my tone I explained, "The UK stands for United *Kingdom* and not United *States*, so the laws are actually different, Susie," I said.

"It's Susan," she replied with a little edge.

Go ahead, I thought, get edgy – I'll meet you there.

"I mean to say," she continued, "that the European airports have tons of stairs and don't you think it will be so difficult physically for you both to lug suitcases up and down all those stairs?"

"I do usually like to bring my husband, who doubles as a personal Sherpa, but since we are only taking one rolling bag and one personal item it's not going to be an issue."

"We are?" asked Nancy wide-eyed.

"And, Susie..."

"Susan."

"Sure. The rolling bag we're taking is by REI and it can turn into a backpack should we encounter a long staircase so we actually have it all figured out. But thank you for helping us to identify yet another possible negative."

"Oh," she said with a fake grin and squinty eyes. "Certainly."

As we walked away, I saw Nancy looked a little pale.

"Hey, I'm sorry. There is just something almost hyena-like about that that woman. You know, sitting in the weeds, hoping for a kill she can live off of?"

"Deborah, that's a little dramatic."

"The only analogy that came to me."

"But about the carry-on thing, you're just annoying her, right? You don't really think we can go away for a couple of weeks with one small suitcase?"

So maybe I have a reputation as a woman who is still

wearing the jeans she bought in 1975, but that's not true. Those jeans fell apart last year. I cremated them and they sit in an urn on the mantle — sometimes I light a candle.

"Nancy, I am serious. We need practical and comfortable. It's only the two of us. I'm thinking two pair of jeans, a pair of stretch sweats, several shirts, raincoat, done."

"I'm thinking I am traveling to a foreign country and I want clean clothing and options. I want to be prepared."

"For what?"

"For whatever?"

"Won't it be awesome to travel light and not worry about those things?"

"Won't it be awesome to have something clean and appropriate to wear no matter what we encounter?"

"But if we check luggage, you know the airlines will probably lose our luggage, and we'll be moving around so much it might be hard to catch up with us. We won't be tied down by anything this way. And there will be extra baggage fees. Let's do this like we expect to plan a lot of future trips. I really want to travel light. We need to be flexible, not fashionable."

"What if we need something nice?"

"For what? It's only you and me. We've watched each other give birth, really, we've already seen the worst."

Perhaps Nancy wasn't thrilled with this, but to her credit she went online and began a rigorous, thorough investigation to locate the absolute largest allowable carry-on. She compared inches, centimeters, compartments, volume numbers, and could quote passages from *Consumer Reports*. She's impressive when she's on a mission.

For my part, I promised to take a packing lesson online, which I did. After a little research and experimentation, I became a packing sage. I learned to get a jaw-dropping number of things into a carry-on. It was the closest I've ever come to enjoying geometry. After several attempts, I decided to go with the counter-intuitive rolling method. Nancy was stunned at the amount of clothing I pulled out of my suitcase, which I found satisfying since she is so inherently organized.

Nancy liked a plan. I liked no plan. We decided we would do the research, plan the trip, but we would be ready to change course at any moment providing we could stomach the added expense.

Nancy had one non-negotiable desire, which was to attend a cookery school (I didn't know cookery was a word). She wanted to learn some local cooking tips and to create some interesting new recipes based on our travels. She didn't want to return home to cook the same family meals when it was going to be only the two of them. Change was needed; she would find a new kind of comfort food. Nancy was also committed to creating some new cocktails based on some classic Irish ingredients. I didn't know my sister had this latent chef urge, but I was personally psyched about the cocktail idea.

So, along with Nancy's non-negotiable desire for the cookery school, I also had one non-negotiable desire, which was to sleep in an authentic medieval castle, to live inside that history and touch the same stone that had been touched by fingers of people gone a millennium ago; to imagine what went on inside their heads, what their lives were like, what their families were like, what they wished for, dreamt about. We committed ourselves to achieving each one of our two non-negotiable goals and they turned out to be the most entertaining moments of our trip, albeit not in the way we expected. We agreed that our most important ambition was to unearth the buried carefree wilder selves we lost after we skidded into domesticity and wound-up exhausted and paralyzed holding a jar of peanut butter and staring bleary-eyed at some kid's essay on Thomas Jefferson.

In the planning stage, it occurred to me that while Nancy and I had raised our kids very differently, there was a defining echo of personality in the way we were each approaching this trip. Nancy liked structure. As a mother, she had a road map in her mind and she was most comfortable, and most successful, with organized house rules and proscribed expectations. To my mind, she was strict. She may have inherited this from our parents whose motto was: "If there's no rule then the answer is no." Inherent or not, Nancy was at ease with rules – she saw them as a tool. Rules give me hives. Once my kids passed about nine years old everything was up for negotiation. Yes, this could cause chaos, and at least one odd moment when, after an evening out with her 15-year-old friends, Anna burst into our bedroom where Larry was doing the TV up-up-down-down-up and she demanded a curfew.

"Wait, what?" I asked dumbfounded.

"All my friends have a curfew!"

"You *want* a curfew?"

My sisters and I had a curfew/bedtime set in cement when we were growing up. Sometimes, if my parents were going out, they would tell the babysitter (who we had well into our teens) that we could stay up half an hour later and it was cause for jubilation. What did curfews teach me? Curfews taught me how to quietly climb out my bedroom window.

"All my friends know exactly what their timing is each weekend," she replied petulantly – because is there anything on earth more cosmically petulant than a 15-year-old girl?

"But every weekend is different. Why do you want a set rule? Why can't we approach each evening individually?"

"No. I want to know exactly in advance."

"Um...okay?"

Nonplussed, my husband and I gave her a curfew. Then, we extended it to her twin brother and younger sister as well, because, well, otherwise it was just weird.

Underneath the rule–no rule dilemma, Nancy and I, like most moms, had uncompromising drive to put our kids' plans and lives first, no matter how inconvenient or inglorious. Our children, five in all, extremely different kids by nature, raised by very different methods, all turned out pretty well (so far) and with strong ties to each other, which leads me to surmise that there are a lot of good ways to raise children, and it's harder to screw them up than we were led to believe. Perhaps the patronizing experts who populate the media, write the parenting books, lecture at the schools, and those other mothers who roll their eyes in disapproval because they hold the secret to perfect motherhood should chill a bit. And with those moms in mind, I would like to suggest that avoiding conversations with them as they faux-complained about how wearisome it is to raise their *gifted* children, while still keeping my place in the carpool lane, should be an Olympic event. I concocted a series of elaborate avoidance techniques surely worthy of some kind of medal. I repeatedly sprayed my windshield cleaner fluid and ran the wipers for visual obfuscation; I flipped down the visor and lifted up my body to hide my face behind it; I buried my head in a book; I kept on huge sunglasses even in the rain and wore headphones attached to nothing; or I pretended to be arguing on my cell phone. Sometimes I would lie down flat in the driver's seat, just to avoid hearing one more parent of a four-year-old tell me how gifted their child was. It is amazing how many of those gifted children turned into subhuman teenagers. Really, they did, I know every one of those kids. But I digress, and maybe rant, just a little, but only because we've *all* been trapped at Back To School Night with *that* mom.

Personal styles aside, fundamentally Nancy and I were agreed, that as far as this adventure was concerned, we were free and we decided that we would be devoted to trying every cocktail from Dublin to Wicklow, and to chat-up every stranger who glanced our way. There was a world outside of our homes and we were longing to fill our lives with newness. At this transition, we felt two conflicting emotions: on the one hand, pitifully empty inside that our children were gone, and on the other hand, a bit like we were getting out of prison and really nervous about it.

Of course, Ireland has more then its share of kick-ass independent women for us to emulate as we set our course. As far back as Mebh, (pronounced Mave) a story from the 1st century that tells the tale of a husband and wife who got into a bragging match about who had more wealth, and which one of them had married up. Surely plenty of contemporary married couples tease each other this way, but Mebh and hubby took it a bit further and actually did an inventory, laying-out every single thing each of them had. When it came down to the final accounting, as it turned out, Mebh was one fertile bull short of victory. Being a ballsy Irish woman, and not about to be bested by her man, Mebh set-out to borrow a bull from a neighbor, offering as payment for the loan some livestock and "her own friendly thighs", which seemed exceedingly neighborly to me. I know I've borrowed a few things: sugar, corn syrup, and milk from my neighbor, and frankly, it never occurred to me to offer my friendly thighs, and I'm fairly certain my neighbors are damn glad I didn't. Unfortunately, Mebh's negotiations for the bull broke down, at which point, annoyed, she raised a huge army and led them against the neighbor in bloody battle, sword in hand. Now, I have seen my own share of battles, mostly with the wireless phone companies, but I have yet to take up arms.

The thread of dynamic Irish women continued throughout the centuries. Constance Markievicz (born Gore-Booth) who was raised in County Sligo, where our mother's family comes from, founded the suffrage movement there and went on to participate in the revolutionary uprising against the British in 1916. With a gun in hand, alongside the men, she fought for Irish independence. This was a gun-toting, pants wearing, child bearing woman-and-a-half. She was sentenced to death for her activities during the rebellion. Her sentence was commuted since they couldn't get their heads around executing a woman, and she spent years imprisoned before the amnesty that set her free, after which she became the first Irish woman elected to Parliament. Inspirational.

This tradition of formidable Irish women continues today. Both the seventh and eighth presidents of Ireland have been women. The first was Mary Robinson who was president from 1990 – 1997, and who then went on to serve as the United Nations high commissioner for human rights from 1997- 2002; and the second, Mary McAleese (Mary's a big name in this Catholic country), took the presidency in 1997. And, yes, just when Nancy and I were feeling like superwomen, we learned that both women have law degrees, husbands, and children. Like I said, kick-ass.

There were lots of reasons to be impressed by the force of will and personal power of the women of Ireland. Our mom's grandmother ran away from her home in Sligo (oh, I guess it runs in the family). She stole away in the middle of the night fleeing an arranged marriage. She took one look at that 60-year-old man they were pawning her off on and split. She jumped on a ship leaving for the United States. The family hired a man to track her down and bring her back, but she outran him. She made the trip across the Atlantic crammed into the ship's lower hold with many other Irish scrounging for food and water on the long voyage. She was processed with them through Ellis Island and got a job as a maid with a local family for room and board. Thus began, on U.S. soil, the link of babies that led to us, and then to our own babies, who had the unmitigated gall to grow up on us, at which point we needed to leave the country and head for Ireland. There's something appealingly cyclical about all of that.

So, in keeping with the plucky women stock Nancy and I were descended from, we decided to toss caution aside, ignore all the dire warnings, and...yes, rent a car. We would go and we would drive on the wrong side of the road. Whoo hoo. Okay, it's not armed rebellion, or a post at the U.N., but we had to start somewhere. Besides, practically speaking, driving would be more cost effective by eliminating taxis and trains, and it would give us all the flexibility we craved. One of the elements of motherhood we were looking to leave behind was the ruthless scheduling: breakfast, carpool, school, dance, volleyball, little league, soccer, school play rehearsal, dinner, homework, and that was just one day. The timing matrix of motherhood had been unrelenting. We needed a spreadsheet to get everyone where they needed to be. So with the unyielding nature of those chauffeur years in mind, we agreed no plan was set in stone. Initially, we decided we would spend a few days in Dublin, drive directly west across the entire country to Galway. Proceed from Galway to Clifton. Then, turn south along the coast past the Cliffs of Moher, east to Cork, from Cork north to Wicklow, and back to Dublin.

Nancy had located an established cooking school in Wicklow called Ballyknocken to satisfy her one requirement, and after hours and hours of detailed research we had found a castle to spend the night in an hour west of Galway in Clifton. Many of the castles turned hotels were really pricey and the pictures of this place looked dramatic and historic and the price was reasonable.

Nancy and I purchased our respective airline tickets-to-ride and then focused on where we might stay. We spent tens of hours on the web searching for the exact right hotel in each location. I was desperate for authenticity and was willing to sacrifice anything for it; Nancy was desperate for proper bedding. Since my insomnia is so dreadful I never expect to sleep well so bed construction and linen thread count is usually not something I think about. It is not true that I don't notice a comfortable bed, I do, I just don't look for it, don't even consider it, when choosing a place to stay. On the other hand, Nancy had a laser sharp eye for evaluating the comfort of any prospective hotel from the passport-sized photo of the bed on the web page. The first click on any hotel website was to the picture of the guest room. With just a glance Nancy could dissect the beds, the sheets, the pillows, the quilt, and if pressed the viability of the black-out drapes. She was adamant that without a firm mattress, a thick mattress pad, and soft pillows she would be no good to anyone the next day. She wanted to get up every day rested and ready. Sleep matters, she would say, especially if you're traveling. I figured based on the possibility of blood curdling screaming, it was probably wise to get her exactly what she needed to sleep soundly.

"What about this hotel?" I asked.

"Are you kidding, look at those beds?

"What? They look okay. They look like...beds."

"Nope. Check-out the depth of that pathetic mattress, and look at the cases on those pillows. The fabric is shiny. Shiny means coarse, rough, nasty. And this is their best foot forward. They think they can fool us with those puffed-up throw pillows, well not likely. And just because we are going to see medieval structures doesn't mean we have to sleep on the rack."

I learned over time that Nancy's gift for assessing the comfort level of any bed based on these tiny photos was uncanny, truly bordering on the occult.

FLYING AWAY

Nancy and I live near different airports so we were meeting in Dublin.

For me, every time they close the cabin doors on these jumbo jets I look out the window skeptically and a little voice inside of me screams – run.

I understand little planes; they make sense to me. It seems reasonable that a little plane might be able to take-off and stay aloft. It feels fly-able. But these things? These massive weighty metal behemoths? Every time they go barreling down the runway I'm convinced it will never take-off in time. It does not seem possible. Of course, it also does not seem possible to me that the Earth is hurling through space at 18 miles a second, or that my hairdryer works because energy that I cannot see comes racing through a tiny wire. I have a tacit understanding with electrons: I will believe in them as long as they keep my lights on. So, when the flight attendant closed the cabin doors on this monstrosity of a jumbo jet, I closed my eyes and trusted science. It has never let me down.

Ah, the romance of flight: your knees jammed-up

against the seat in front of you, hungry, either freezing or burning alternately, with some phlegmatic stranger breathing on you and some selfish traveler tilting their chair all the way back into your face. What can compare with the mind-screeching claustrophobia, the surly attendants, the cranky babies, the carts blocking your path to the bathroom and then blocking your way back from the bathroom, the static filled movies that cost a fortune, and the person in the next seat so close you can feel their arm hair up against your shirt as you engage in a covert war to maintain armrest domination? Hour after hour, the air in the plane gets dryer, your throat is sticking together because the attendants are too busy, or too chatty, to get you water, and you'd sell your soul for chapstick.

Of course, I suppose, looking back there were worse flights; when my twins were two years old we flew to St. Louis from San Diego to visit their grandparents. It had to happen, how could we not visit? And even though I was six months pregnant, we figured there were two of us; it was man-to-man coverage - how bad could it be? It was only going to get harder after that third baby came along.

I would like to go on record here apologizing to everyone on that plane that day. Now, it was not our fault that the plane sat on the runway for five hours (remember when the airlines did that) turning a four-hour trip into a nine-hour trip. I don't even feel it was our fault when we were subjected to a sanitary crisis, ran out of diapers, and needed to have the flight attendant make a loud announcement begging for supplies. (Thank you whoever you were.) But when my two-year-old daughter started screaming, for reasons that escape me to this day, and even though I am thoroughly confident everyone on that plane felt like screaming, I suppose we, as her genetic donors, were somehow responsible for her lungs and her shocking stamina. And since we could not stop her, distract her, bribe her, or threaten her, with any success, I rushed her into one of the bathrooms in the back of the plane, slammed the door, and stayed there for over two hours with her uncomfortably balanced on my pregnant belly, sandwiched into that cramped metal room, with her screaming at the top of her lungs. I still start to sweat when I think about it. I was crying. She was crying. It is a Top Ten Worst Moment memory. Ah, good times.

DUBLIN & BEYOND THE PALE

Ireland is about the same size as South Carolina. If you portion off The Republic of Ireland (eliminating a small northern chunk of the island which is part of the UK) you've got a pretty small country. Dublin is the capital city and where over 1/3 of the total population of 4.5 million live. The median age is 34 – it's a young crowd, which kind of appealed to us, and may be why so many people have this "young place" mindset when it comes to Ireland. Ireland actually has an exceedingly long tale of human history. There is a megalithic passage tomb in County Meath, north of Dublin, called Newgrange, which historians date at about 3200 BCE, which means it pre-dates the Great Pyramid of Giza and Stonehenge by about 600 years, give-or-take. The mound complex lays out over an acre of Irish countryside with a white stone front and stone chambers. What is most captivating about Newgrange happens every year on December 21st. On the winter solstice, as the sun rises, it lines up with a hole in the roof and a shaft of light brightens the entire inside of the stone chamber for 17 minutes. Now, that's a wonder. Who wouldn't want to see that? To secure a spot for the viewing of this event, you need to apply. People are chosen by lottery. So, that's very fair. In 2010 there were 25,349 applications and in September they pulled 50 names. Right, 50. Do you feel lucky? Nancy and I found a really terrific tour of Newgrange (music and all) compliments of YouTube.

We met at Dublin airport, hugged, and hailed a cab for the celebrated Shelbourne Hotel, which we were not certain we should have spent the money on, but we were heading for nonetheless. It wasn't outrageous and even on a budget it was an extravagance we decided we could manage.

At some point, all mothers spend money on something they shouldn't, it's just rarely on themselves; more often it is that one pretty (ridiculously expensive) little formal dress for their daughter's first high school dance, because she feels gawky and ugly and unlovable and pleads with her eyes when she sees it on the rack. The whole rest of the week you are running a news crawl in your head: "Oh I can't believe I paid for that dress." And then, the night comes, and she wobbles down the stairs, all knobby knees and long hair, with too much eye make-up and unstable on a pair of heels that look like they came from the Playboy mansion, and bright toenails painted a color not found in nature. She searches your eyes for confidence because the pimpled boy with the braces and the supermarket corsage is standing in the hallway, in his brother's hand-me-down suit and the tennis shoes he thought he could get away with because they were black. And you look up at your little girl and see that she feels beautiful in that dress, and no matter what it cost it was worth every dime. Seeing that shaky confidence on her fresh face you admit you'd get a night job to pay for that dress – oh, wait, you're a mom, you already have a night job.

It was a little over a half an hour ride from the airport to the center of Dublin. There were no looming skyscrapers to overwhelm like in so many U.S. cities. The buildings were mostly three or four stories, and lively. Many were a rosy old brick, and others were painted yellow, or vivid green. We passed one building that was a neon turquoise color with peach trim, and a few with screaming red doors. At each of the major intersections, a cautionary canary yellow, large diamond-shaped patchwork laid out over the entire center of the crossing area. All this color was endearing and felt warmly welcoming to us. Some of the streetlights were very old, beautifully carved with swan-like necks, and others were contemporary and so that uninspired bland colorless metal. There were Dubliners going about their day, walking and riding bicycles, and yes, we gulped when the driver took a hard left turn and swung into what we would consider the oncoming lane of traffic. I looked over at Nancy and she had closed her eyes. (This should have been my first clue that Nancy was going to have a wee bit of an adjustment when I started driving.)

"Leprechaun."

"What?"

"Open your eyes, you're missing Ireland."

"This driving situation is challenging."

"You just have to flip everything around in your brain and think backwards."

"Thanks, Deborah, that really clears it up."

The taxi driver spoke up, "Where you girls from?"

This was the first time I looked inside the cab and I noticed there were about eight No Smoking signs aimed at us: on the windows, on the back of the front seats, pasted just above and below both door handles, and hanging from the rear view mirror.

So I said, "Okay if I smoke?"

An incredulous pause.

Then, Nancy jumped in, "She's kidding."

"Oh," he said. "Yeah, well you might think so, I'd say."

"What?" I looked at Nancy, "What did he say?"

Nancy answered him, "We're from California." Nancy always engages with people, which is an extraordinary trait. I prefer to be left to my own thoughts and wish they'd stop talking to me.

"Ah, your first trip here, then?"

"Yes. Actually our grandmother's family came from here."

"Yup, everyone's got a little Irish in them. It's what happens when half the folk run away to keep from eating grass and starving to death."

"Okay," I said dryly, "Not here long enough for that much reality, still working off the faerie, castle, wee people, concept."

The taxi crossed over a thin muddy Liffey River and headed south toward the hotel. Here we were. Dublin. We had simply decided to go – and we did. Everything was fresh, every one of my senses was activated, and while it was exactly what we needed, I couldn't shake the feeling that there was something I should be doing.

"I feel like I forgot something," I whispered to Nancy.

"Me, too. Like I forgot to feed the dog, or left the shower on."

"Unnerving."

"It's as though my unconscious is still trying to line-up chores and do all of the things it has been doing all these years."

"I think we're going to have to put a major effort into letting go of home."

A conscious effort to relax was going to be required. It reminded me of the time my husband bought me a massage as a birthday gift. I arrived, disrobed, and lay face down on the table as requested. The masseuse entered and (in what was clearly her "inside voice") told me to relax completely. I should let my thoughts unwind like in a running stream, and so immediately that stream suggestion made me have to pee again, which only got worse after she put on the tape of the ocean waves.

Relax, she said, let your thoughts unwind: *An hour really will I be here for an hour lying still getting nothing done because if you really want to relax me what I need is for this strong-armed masseuse to run a few useful errands like a trip to supermarket or a swing past the drug store because I know my son needs construction paper and I think I've bought colored pencils about four hundred times and they're never around and what the hell happens to the scotch tape in my house are they eating it and what was with that flier the school sent home about telling the kids not to sniff glue I'm really sure my kids would not ever have thought to do that it if they hadn't mentioned it in the flier which basically gives them the idea that other kids are doing it which feels a little like permission and I think I forgot to sign that permission slip for the field trip tomorrow and tomorrow is garbage day so I have to rinse out that gooey disgusting recycling bin and I now know I can't recycle those light-up sneakers because of the mercury and I need to get new sneakers in that new place that opened when I pick up the dry cleaning and maybe I can walk the dog there and someone has to wash that dog and I need to wash the vegetables for dinner but not the mushrooms because you're supposed to brush the dirt off the mushrooms and not wet them down and I did read somewhere that leaving the skin on the cucumber might be hard for digestion but is actually good because there are nutrients in the skin and I need to remember where I put that nu-*

skin bandage thing I bought so I can get it on that blister
and I'm not letting her wear those rolling shoes any more
shoes should not roll and even though they want those
fruit roll-ups it's like rubber sugar and how could sticky
sugar be good for their teeth and ... "Okay, your hour is
up. How do you feel?"

"What?"

In the cab, I turned to Nancy, "Are you sure there
isn't there something I'm supposed to be doing right
now?"

"You're doing it."

"Kind of strange."

"What's strange is how unreachable we are, you
know?"

For moms who were hyper-vigilant about their kids'
crisis coverage — moms who left phone numbers, and
back-up plans, and emergency tree info, in case we
were momentarily unavailable like, say, getting a hair
cut or pap smear (good times); for those moms, the ones
who should be running FEMA because they have trian-
gulated the crap out of any and all possible emergency
situations, the ones who wrote the home phone number
in magic marker on the inside of their kid's arm when
they were on a kindergarten field trip, yeah, we know
who we are – it was going to take a forced separation,
like perhaps 6,000 miles of distance, 3,000 of which
was open ocean, and a minimum 8 hour time change to
successfully reprogram.

"What time is it?" I asked.

"About noon, I guess," Nancy responded.

"Ireland's eight hours ahead, so it's four a.m. in California."

Nancy's eyes shone with mischief, "Guess we're out
past curfew."

"How do you feel about that?"

"Mischievous – good – and also mildly panicked."

"Me, too."

The Shelbourne came into view up ahead. It was a breathtaking, red brick and stucco, an eight-story beauty built in 1824, thoughtfully renovated, and now owned by Marriott (which bummed me out for unidentifiable reasons). Originally, the Shelbourne was a cluster of three adjoining Georgian townhouses. A man named Martin Burke bought them and turned them into this hotel. The hotel sits across the street from St. Stephen's Green, and is just a couple of blocks from the shops and restaurants on famous Grafton Street promenade. Stephen's Green is a 22-acre rectangular park in the middle of Dublin, attractively landscaped with a small lake, several memorials, and an old-fashioned bandstand. Before the trees and the Sunday afternoon strollers, Stephen's Green had a rather sinister history. The park hosted lepers in medieval times. Later, barracks stood there, where imprisoned rebels were tortured, and the gallows that were erected near the corner hanged many an unlucky Irishman and one infamous Irishwoman, Darkey Kelly, who is now known as Ireland's first serial killer after they found a number of dead bodies in the basement of her house of ill-repute. (And I thought my house was unkempt.) The Green was also the center point of the Easter Rising and war for independence of 1916. I understand the ladies having high tea at the Shelbourne had to dodge stray bullets, really so déclassé.

The Shelbourne doorman, in a Jiminy Cricket top hat, swung open our cab door and welcomed us. One look at this lovely place and we knew we were going to have to watch every cost. We had only just begun our trip and we had chosen the most expensive place. And even though we had negotiated a really good rate, we were cognizant of being thrifty and so we waved off the bellhop, yes, a small consideration, but at the very least we could roll our own bags. (I was feeling smugly vindicated for the carry-on directive, at least, at this moment.) We yanked out our airline approved "one carry-on and one personal item" and rolled toward the revolving half-wood, half-glass front door. Nancy was ahead of me; she stepped in confidently pulling her bag behind her, and came to a jarring stop. The door jammed. The space was not wide enough to accommodate a traveler plus their rolling luggage, and an edge of her suitcase caught. She was wedged in like a human doorstop. Jiminy Cricket darted around trying to extricate Nancy, who stood looking out of the pie-shaped glass cubicle with that you-have-got-to-be-kidding-me look on her face. The revolving door wouldn't budge in either direction. I thought Jiminy was going to blow a fuse – he was clearly not trained for this contingency – a guest was stuck! On his watch. Poor guy was frantic. A general alarm was raised and a number of Jiminy Crickets arrived on the scene, each one apologizing and industriously maneuvering the door back and forth in a valiant attempt to free my sister. I scooted through the side entrance and waited for her on the other side of the revolving door inside the lobby. I supposed guests didn't carry their own bags through the revolving door and into a hotel like this, but rather glided in blithely with their wallets opened and leaving the luggage to luggage-people who pulled them through the other door. Our eyes met through the glass, she cocked her head and shrugged. When we were little girls our dad used to sing a Frank Sinatra song to her: "Nancy With The Laughing Face." Yeah, I remembered that just then. When my sister had finally been publicly extricated from the front door of the hotel we let the porter take our bags and we walked into the front lobby.

It is so curious how people change in relationship to where they happen to be. We become different people in different places. This is particularly true for mothers who need to play so many different roles. At the County Fair we're that BBQ eating, Ferris Wheel riding, flip flop wearing woman trailing three kids elbows deep in ice cream; at the School Board meeting we're the blazer-wearing, hair-tied-back businesswoman with a few pointed questions about the Standard Tests they keep trying to jam down our un-standard kids; and if there were a place that would elicit the ever-lovin' elegance out of you, it was the Shelbourne. This was a graceful hotel with white marble, gold and red fabrics, wrought iron railings, and exquisite furniture. A magnificent black iron and dark wood banister curved up the grand staircase from the lobby floor. We felt different walking through here, passing the gravity defying floral displays on various tables. The Lord Mayor's Lounge was on our right and No. 27 bar on the left. Through the entrance hall we passed into a second foyer where the front desk was situated along the right wall. There was a pretty sitting area to the left, in case, you wanted to rest your feet, and several happy clerks were smiling from the desk area waiting to assist us. This was as civilized as one might expect to find.

I didn't really focus on a single thing the front desk lady was saying as we checked-in, I was too charmed by her accent. Those of us old enough to recall that Irish Spring commercial should admit that we ran out and bought that soap as soon as the cute guy started talking. What is it about the Irish accent that makes us want to throw our arms around these people? I was standing there grinning and enjoying her adorable speech right up until she said, "And it's 20 euro per day for the Internet."

"What?" Now she had my attention.

"Twenty." She smiled and then held out a platter, "Brownie?"

"That's about 35 dollars?" I blurted out.

"Freshly baked." Still holding out the platter.

Nancy asked politely, "Every day? Twenty, each?"

"Oh, no," she replied still smiling and not looking half as adorable.

Nancy looked for a bright side, "So, we'll split it."

"Twenty for only one computer," she explained.

"I don't understand."

"Only one computer can sign-on per room. Sure you wouldn't like a brownie?"

I tried to make sense of this. "There are two people. We both have computers. We both need to use."

"Yes, I see, but only one computer per room."

And now I'm feeling a lot less Lucky Charms about this hotel. I tried reason. "That's like telling us only one of us can use the hairdryer while we're here."

She smiled huge, "Sorry that's just the way our Internet is set-up."

Nancy took over. With her enviable cucumber cool and a sweet smile she said, "You know computers are no longer luxuries."

"Yes, well..." the clerk shifted a little in her shoes.

I said, "It's how we pay our bills." Now, we were sisters on a roll finishing each other's sentences.

"And how we know where to go and how to get there..."

"It's how we check on our kids..."

"And communicate with our friends..."

"And get important messages..."

"From the airlines..."

"Or our banks..."

"Or credit card companies..."

"It is how we manage most of the elements of our lives..."

"We need to both be in the room and check our messages and respond..."

"At the same time."

The clerk stared a little wide-eyed. "I'll make management aware of your comments."

Nancy and I looked at each other stymied. Nancy leaned in quietly to me and said, "We need to let this go."

"I'm lost without my computer." I could hear the whine in my whisper.

"So, we're lost. We were going to learn to roll with it, remember?"

"Um."

"Deborah, roll."

"Rolling is against my nature."

"Roll."

"Right." We both turned back to the desk lady and smiled, although I'm sure the struggle was clear in my eyes.

Computers have become intimate objects in our lives. Where I might think nothing of lending my cellphone, or my even my mascara, handing over my computer for someone else to use, anyone else, well, that feels revealing, as though I'm letting someone look into my brain and the intimacies of my life without a filter. Note to hotels: figure this out. What was most surprising to us was that during our travels the more budget a hotel was the more apt we were to have unlimited wi fi in the room. The more expensive a hotel, and we had to pay, sometimes every day, for access.

Waiting for the Shelbourne elevator (which was nicer than my living room) I saw a small table with a glass top. Underneath the glass, the hotel had put some very old letters from guests of the hotel. They were yellowed and craggy edged and looking at them I gasped. I'm embarrassingly thrilled by old letters from dead people – go figure. While Nancy was commenting intelligently on the style and craftsmanship of the little table while I was glued to the crumbled missives from people I don't know, to other people I don't know, for reasons I, yeah, don't know.

We entered our hotel room through a little hall with a big closet on the right and a marble bathroom on the left. Inside the main area were two crisp white double beds. The carpet under our feet was spongy and sweetly yielding. The main drapes were pulled open and stacked voluminously on either side of the large window, revealing a gossamer curtain that filtered the light coming in through the windows to a buttery softness where even after 20 hours traveling we looked good. The desk, dresser and nightstand shined in a rich glossy wood. The room was flawless and impeccably clean.

Clean is not something I've seen a lot of these last 20 child-raising years. Not that I didn't fight for it. I fought, cajoled, pleaded, and lost. I'd been in other women's houses and lots of them were clean and it just made me mad. Why couldn't that be me? Why? I could not figure out what I was doing wrong? My sister-in-law's home was suspiciously spotless, otherworldly clean, and sometimes I was so jealous, and other times I knew they must have been pretending to live there. It didn't seem to matter how I threatened my kids they were incapable of complying. I kept telling myself "pick your battles," and then I'd walk into the kitchen, see the mess, and hit the wall. I decided I could live with it if only I could keep the kitchen uncluttered. I designated the kitchen counter as the Throw Out Counter and I called it exactly that for months. "Oh, look what's on the Throw Out Counter." "Oh, this shouldn't be on the Throw Out Counter." One day, in explosive frustration, bordering on lunacy, and after years of demands, I threw in the garbage every single thing they'd left on the Throw Out Counter including homework, DVDs, and clothing.

"Mom, where are my volleyball shoes?"

"Did you leave them on the Throw Out Counter?"

"My math homework."

"Did you leave it on the Throw Out Counter? Guess *why* it's called that?"

And I'll admit to a deeply satisfying moment when I saw them rifling panicked through the trash can later.

I had a neighbor who told me she would walk through the house with a plastic bag, throw everything in it, tie it up, and leave it in the garage. I tried this, too. My girls, Anna and Olivia, went berserk ripping open bags at the last minute before dressing for school and tossing stuff all over the garage floor, while my little boy, Jeff, worked his way down to one t-shirt and one pair of shorts, which he then calmly began wearing every single day without a second thought. This is one of those mother trade-offs that felt unfair. I wanted my kids to be happy, and I wanted clean, never quite accepting that, for my family, this was an either/or situation. And, as they grew, there were the other trade-offs – harder ones.

My girls began making their beds fairly quickly, but Jeff, well, not so much. So, in the morning, after I dropped him at school, I would make his bed. Arriving back at the grammar school later for pick-up, I would walk onto the playground his eyes would light up and he would run into my arms. It was one of the glorious mommy moments that sustained me, that little boy hug with just a tinge of desperation. I could never understand the mothers who sat in the cars and waited for their little ones to be loaded by the teachers. Once we were on our way home I would remind him, "You didn't make your bed again today, Jeffrey. That is your responsibility." And he would look distantly out the window or pinch one of his sisters just for fun. I wondered if it would ever happen, and then, one day, it was a Thursday, I walked into his bedroom and he'd done it! His bedspread was pulled up taut and his bear sat on top. *Oh, isn't he wonderful,* I thought. I was rich with pride and excitement. I was going to take him for ice cream straight from school. I pulled into the lot, got out, and strode onto the playground. There he was. He saw me. I squatted down as he approached ready for my hug, but a new expression crossed his face. His step was anxious. His eyes darted back and forth to the other boys on the playground and as he approached he whispered in a panic, "Don't, Mom. Don't touch me." And he strutted on by me, his little boy body rigid with phony detachment. I stood up bewildered by his sudden embarrassment. Then, I remembered the perfectly made bed and I was wounded by this unanticipated trade-off. I didn't realize that old enough to make his bed meant beyond the age I could hug him in public. Mommy hugging could not happen in front of the other little tough grammar school boys in their Batman T-shirts. Now, when I picked him up, I needed to keep a little distance. No more running into my arms? It was an unthinkable trade that I would never have made if I'd had a choice. Screw the bed. He would not hug me again in public until he entered high school.

That Thursday night, alone in the darkened kitchen, while the baked macaroni and cheese pan soaked in the sink, I sat down on the kitchen stool and thought about how much I was going to miss that hug, and how

I wished I would have seen that trade-off coming. Larry came in.

"What are you doing in the dark?"

"Thinking."

"Oh, I knew I smelled something burning."

"Funny."

"What's wrong?"

"It's silly."

"No doubt. But tell me anyway."

"Jeffrey..."

"Yeah?"

"Jeffrey made his bed."

Larry was unsure how to react to this because it appeared that somehow this was bad news, but he couldn't figure out how. So he said, "That's good, right? He's growing up, right?"

Yup, poor Larry, absolutely the wrong thing to say.

At the Shelbourne, Nancy looked out the window of our room. "This room is spotless. Deborah, do you remember, when we were growing up that Mom would vacuum the house every single day?"

"I do. Some carpet salesman told her it was the only way to keep her carpet pristine and she went for it. Dad used to say 'Model home – it needs to look like a model home'."

"I think that comes from growing up poor. They were both a tad excessive when it came to taking care of the house."

"Next to them I'm relaxed," I joined Nancy at the window and stared out at Dublin.

"And on the weekends?" Nancy plopped down on the bed. "Dad would hand out the chores and no one wanted to do pick-up."

"Ah! Remember pick-up?"

Pick-up was when one of us would crawl down the hallway and staircase picking-up little pieces of lint with our fingers so there was not a spec to be seen on the carpet. At the time, it seemed normal, but it was one of those childhood things you look back on later and wonder — what were they thinking?

We three sisters kept our rooms clean to Marine Corps standards, or else there were real consequences. So for my kids who couldn't seem to keep anything clean, maybe it was because my consequences were never what they should have been, but in my defense, my kids were unusually, some said phenomenally, and others said galactically strong-willed. And my biggest fault in the cause-and-effect department was my complete emotional inability to make them unhappy. Consequences were simply hard for me. (Consequences are the 21st century parents' euphemism for punishment, and it doesn't fool even the most clueless child, who knows perfectly well what punishment feels like, and sees the name game for what it is.) Nancy was much more solid in this area, setting down reasonable rules and sticking to them.

A few times, I did come to wonder if my kids had eyesight issues. I would insist they clean the kitchen after dinner. My husband and I would go for a walk so as to avoid hearing the inevitable intra-sibling accusations and negotiations during that process, and then, when we returned the kitchen would appear clean, but we actually *have* electricity, so I would turn on the lights. This is when things went south. I could see the splotches on the counter top that had not been washed, and the crumbs in the corners of the floor, and the dark slide marks inside the porcelain white sink where they'd pseudo-washed the dinner pot (but not the pot cover, not ever the cover) and the conversation would sound something like this:

"This isn't clean."

Kid response, (any one of them), "Yes, it is."

"You didn't wash the counters."

"Don't need it; they look good."

"They're sticky. Look."

"Well, if you're going to run your hand over it."

"I am. I am going to run my hand over it, but I don't need to because I can *see* it."

"Well, I just don't see it."

I suppose we all see differing levels of dirt and clean. I took a righteous pleasure after my twins went off to college and started complaining about their messy roommates. Yeah, that was sweet. "Really?" I'd say with a purposefully fake tone, "That must be so annoying. Perhaps they just don't see it."

I walked around the Shelbourne guest room and looked out the window. "Can you feel it?" I was excited. "It's so fulfilling to feel the history like this. America is too young to give me this feeling."

"You want to feel something? Feel these sheets." I looked over and Nancy was face down on the bed.

"Good?"

"Did you know that Egyptian cotton no longer guarantees a good sheet, nor does thread count because what really matters is the length of the fiber not the number of fibers? This is a nice firm mattress with luxury sheets. We're going to sleep great." Nancy said all of this without lifting her face off the bed. I was impressed.

"You know, Nance, I wanted to splurge on great sheets so I bought the four-ply and after I washed them it felt like I was sleeping on my hairbrush."

"Amateur. Two-ply or four-ply is a bad thing in sheets – a good thing in toilet paper."

"Oh, so why did they advertise four-ply on the front of the package?"

"Because they know you don't know that."

"They know me so well."

Nancy sprang up and walked to her suitcase and we both unpacked like the mothers we were: hanging the hanging things, folding into drawers the folding things, underwear and socks in one drawer, pants in another, lining up all of our respective toilet articles neatly, each on their own side of the sink. It was a beautiful thing. I mentioned this to Nancy and she told me that actually she doesn't unpack ever. Chip always unpacks all of their clothes when they travel. This was unusual. I know families where women unpack the entire thing, and families like mine where each unpacks their own things, but she is the only one I know where the husband does it all and neatly. I felt a tinge of jealousy.

"Even your bathroom stuff?" I asked.

"Well, no, but everything else."

Now, that's a man I could travel with. Traveling with Larry consists of the haphazard tossing of stuff all over the room, the opening up and leaving of the ironing board in the middle of the room so one must step around it for days, and the scattering of toilet articles on both sides of the sink with no consideration for the symmetry of personal space. One time, the confusion led him to use my toothbrush by mistake and I almost divorced him. Now, when we travel together I wrap and re-wrap the head of my toothbrush in Kleenex after each use so there can be no mistakes. It is an odd journey that we begin with our mates in such physical intimacy and eventually freak out if they touch our toothbrush. I suppose I learned over time that we have a different definition of sanitary. I read once that a woman, who has been married ten years, would rather share a towel with a woman she doesn't know than with her own husband.

Nancy said, "Let's take a little walk, get an early dinner, and make our plan for tomorrow."

"No plan."

"We need some kind of plan," Nancy said.

"Okay, the plan is eat, go to bed, get up, decide in the moment what we feel like. Nancy, for 20 years we have planned every second."

"True. I want to get out there now."

"Me, too."

We exited the Shelbourne, crossed the wide boulevard and made our way to the park. We turned right, and walked down St. Stephen's Green Road. We stopped at the corner, got ready to step off the curb, looked down, and saw in huge bright letters "LOOK RIGHT". Yikes! Traffic was coming the other way. I can't tell you how much our jet-lagged, sleep deprived, North American sensibility appreciated the city of Dublin taking us by the hand this way. And it wasn't only on this particular street next to this famous hotel, but in fact, nearly every street, of any consequence, had advice and warnings written in big letters on the asphalt. This was our first example of what we came to view as the Irish's obsession with signs – and I have to say we were grateful.

We strolled down the sidewalk with the park on our left and attractive walk-ups on our right. We passed two rather well-known restaurants, Bentley's Townhouse and Peploe's, continued walking another block, and found ourselves already at famous Grafton Street. This may have been the greatest advantage to splurging for the Shelbourne as the proximity to charming historic Grafton Street was unbeatable. We noticed as we approached Grafton a little grocery store called Londis. We took a look inside and saw that this would be a great place to pick up some very reasonably priced food to carry along with us, or eat in the park, or even back at the hotel for a quick, simple, inexpensive meal.

Less than an hour later, we were splayed out limply on a sofa in the No. 27 bar in the lobby of the Shelbourne. The travel had sucker-punched us and we had stumbled back to the hotel. We had two fabulous cocktails recommended by the bartender, the contents of which we have no accurate recollection. We sat flaccidly for an indeterminable period of time and then somehow wandered up to the room where we crept between the uber-soft clean (so clean) sheets and fell into a sound sleep, the kind of sleep a mother gets only if she has been anesthetized for surgery. Sweet. Clean. Sleeping... ah.

"Ahhh!" A blood-curdling scream ripped through the quiet room and catapulted me out of bed. One second I was fast asleep and the next I was standing in the middle of the room panting. What? Night? Yes, the middle of the night. Ireland? Yes, Ireland. I looked. Nancy was sitting up in her bed just finishing one long shriek at the top of her lungs.

"What?" I felt terrified. "What, Nancy?"

"Oh, sorry."

"Are you okay?"

"I screamed?"

"Yes."

"Did I wake you?"

"Uh...kinda."

"Chip is so used to it that he just nudges me and tells me to go back to sleep without ever really waking up."

"Very adaptable. A good trait in a marriage."

"God, I wish I could make it stop," Nancy said this with such raw longing and helplessness that I felt it in my gut.

For years we have been careful not to ladle too much emotion onto each other since we are both sensitive and don't want to cause each other concern, but here in the dark it felt differently, like you could tell the deep down truth safely because it would fade away by morning. It was something about the darkness, the quiet, a feeling of being alone and being together at the same time, and also very much about being sisters. We spent many nights sharing a room as little girls while we grew up in our family home in a small wooded New Jersey town. It had been a long time since we were together without our husbands, or children. The tie between sisters who have played together, and fought each other, and split Ring Dings fairly (after much debate) is absolute. And while most of our conversations floated on the surface of our lives now, the truth is always known, and always reachable inside, in a way that it isn't with anyone else. With sisters, it's just different.

"Nancy, why do you scream? Is it a bad dream?"

"No. It's a sensation that wakes me. Somewhere in the middle of my sleeping brain I suddenly feel some man lean over my bed. I open my eyes. I think I see him. He's dressed all in black, he's blurry, and huge, and just leaning over me and I scream."

"That's terrifying."

"Yeah, then it takes forever to fall back to sleep because my heart is pounding."

"When did it start?"

"It was that night."

"Which night."

"When you moved out and left me home *alone* for another few years with mom and dad..."

"I grew up."

"Not an excuse and not forgiven. There was that night. Mom, Dad and I were asleep and the phone rang.

Dad answered."

"Hello?"

"Is this Mr. Serra?"

"It is. Who is this?"

"This is the police department. Sir, are you alone?"

"My wife is here. My daughter is in her room. Why?"

"We need you to come downstairs now. We are at the front door and we need you to let us in."

Dad got out of bed.

"What is it?" Mom asked.

"I don't know. I'll go see. Stay here."

Dad walked downstairs and opened the front door. When he did SWAT officers, in riot gear, yanked him out into the courtyard. He was stunned and he struggled, but they said.

"Mr. Serra, we are chasing a fugitive. We followed him to this street and we believe he may very well be hiding inside your home."

"What!" Dad spun around to go back in and they physically restrained him.

"I'm sorry, sir. We cannot let you back in there."

"Get out of my way. My wife and daughter..."

"Sir, please, what's your wife's first name?" "Eileen."

The SWAT officer stepped into the foyer and yelled up the stairs.

"Eileen? Eileen, could you come down here please."

Mom stood in the bedroom. This was not her husband's voice. She swelled with panic

He repeated, "Eileen, I need you to come down now please."

What could she do? She stepped cautiously to look out into the hallway and as soon as she did two SWAT officers grabbed her and rushed her down the stairs, out the front door, and into the courtyard.

"What's your daughter's name, sir?'

Dad said, "I'm going in!"

"Sir, we do not know if he's holding your daughter at this moment. Please, let us do our job. What's her name?"

Holding Mom, who was terrified and trembling, he said, "It's Nancy. She's in the room at the end of the hall."

"How old?"

"Sixteen."

SWAT officers fanned out at the top of the stairs on either side of the hallway. The got into position, squatted down, and aimed their guns.

"Nancy!" The officer called.

No response.

"Nancy!" The officer yelled loudly. "Come here please."

I listened as Nancy explained. "I woke up hearing someone I didn't know calling my name in the middle of the night. I don't see well without my contacts, and I was groggy, but I got up and walked out of my room and into the hallway. There were big figures all in black, with guns pointed at me, crouched all along the hallway. It was blurry but I could see the weapons and the dark suits and I felt instantly paralyzed and like I couldn't breathe."

"Nancy," he said, "are you alone?"

"I just stood there unable to speak or move. He asked me again really loud, "Are you alone?" I nodded my head. They moved in a flash to me, grabbed me, and raced me downstairs and out into the courtyard to Mom and Dad. I don't even think my feet touched the ground. Then, they methodically combed every room, every closet, every cabinet, every trash can, every bathtub, the entire house before they let us back inside. They thanked us and left. And, Deborah, that is why I scream at night."

"I'm so sorry. I remember that happening but I never really focused on how it must have affected you. Frankly, I'm surprised you don't scream every night."

"It's so embarrassing for me now. When we go away somewhere with friends I'm so nervous that it's going to happen. Sometimes I'll go a really long time not doing it and I always hope it's over, but it never is."

"It's completely understandable. And the scream really wasn't that bad," I lied. "I guess we should get on a bathrobe, someone must be on their way up."

"No one ever comes," Nancy said.

"A woman screams like that in the middle of the night in a public hotel and no one knocks?"

"Nope."

"I find that really disturbing?"

"I'm really sorry I woke you up."

"Hey, don't worry about it. I was only half-asleep anyway. I was lying in bed thinking about how guilty I was feeling."

"Guilty, why?" Nancy asked.

"Honestly, all the hit-the-road bravado aside," I admitted, "I feel guilty about spending the money on this trip, you know, just for me."

"Yeah, so do I."

"It was so impulsive," I said and rolled onto my back.

"Spontaneity is not a luxury we've had much the last 20 years."

I could tell Nancy was on her back and staring up at the ceiling like me. "And all of a sudden here we are in Dublin."

"That's what we wanted though, spontaneity, adventure, a change."

"Right," I said, "I needed to prepare for spontaneity –

there's a paradox for you."

"I feel guilty, too, but it's because we're not reachable for our kids."

"Yeah, when the other kids moved out we were on call for them."

"We've been on call in other people's lives for a very long time," Nancy said.

"That's true. But this time, when our two little ones left, we scrambled our jets and flew to the other side of the world."

"Should we have done that? Should – that word again. Seems to follow me around. Seems I'm always managing the 'shoulds' in my life."

"I know both our girls wanted us to go," I said. "They understood how sad watching them leave was for us. The littlest ones always carry that burden."

"What if they need us?"

"Their dads are there."

"Let's Skype them tomorrow."

"Definitely."

"So," Nancy said, "here we are on this incredibly magical trip, instead of feeling totally free and happy, there's this guilty voice in our heads."

"If anyone else in my family, my husband or my kids, went on a trip like this I'd be genuinely happy for them. It's stupid to feel this way."

"Right. So, what do we do?"

"Fight it," I said.

"Reprogram."

"Moving on is going to be a process."

"I think so."

"Do you think Eileen feels this kind of guilt, too?"

"Probably feels a different kind."

Eileen is our other sister; there are three of us and we're close in age. She was the first born and named after our mother. Little Eileen (as she was always known — and still is) chose a completely different path than we did. Little Eileen is a big deal brilliant financial executive in Manhattan with an expense account, frequent flyer miles, and a very serious job populated by people with lists of letters after their names (MBA, PhD, J.D. etc) Eileen is one of the very few valiantly intrepid women from our generation who took a sledgehammer to that glass ceiling. She opened it up for herself, and for other women to follow. We are incredibly proud of her. We brag about her all the time, since she is our sister, after all. To me, though, her life is too rigidly scheduled. I would be miserable in her world. She would be miserable in mine. So many different ways to make one's life.

"You know, Nancy, I just remembered that famous Tenneva Jordon quote: 'A mother is someone who seeing there is only four pieces of pie and five people promptly announces she never did care for pie.' Is that so perfect?" No response. "Nance?" Quiet. "Nancy?" She was back asleep. Evidently, at night, I am as fascinating to my little sister as I am to my husband, who uses me instead of Ambein; he says I'm safer, though much more expensive.

GOOD MORNING, DUBLIN

The Shelbourne is pretty in the morning — airy, bright, and everyone is smiling. They put out some fruit, cookies, and water bottles for the early risers who jog around Stephens Green making the rest of us feel like slugs. Nancy and I took off into the fresh Irish air to meet up with Sandeman Tours. They offer free walking tours in a number of European cities. The quality is usually good for two reasons: firstly, because frequently they are young guides, not yet jaded by the sites and alive with a youthful perspective; and secondly, since they work only for tips they really do try and entertain. Our guide was charming and off-beat and exactly the same age as our sons, which meant we not only intended to tip him very big, but also felt obligated to tell him he was due for a haircut. As we walked toward Dublin Castle, Nancy quizzed him with gentle curiosity about his future goals, and encouraged him, and I believe actually convinced him, to return to college. She has skills.

We were an interesting little group of travelers: a British teacher who was clearly dragging his wife around as she announced loudly she didn't care for tours, for walking, for history, or for the Irish – awkward. There were a few folks on the tour as singles. And several teenagers squarely in the "other" gender category who looked like they had had a great time *last* night, red-eyed and disoriented. And then, there was Paulo and his wife/nurse. Okay, so here's a thought. If you travel to a foreign place, and if you decide to join a number of other people who have also traveled a great distance to a foreign place, and you choose a walking tour, it would be best for everyone if you could, oh, I don't know, walk? What are you thinking if you join a walking tour and you do about ten steps a minute? This guy, who I'm sure was a lovely man, hobbled and tipped over, and couldn't get up even the slightest incline, which meant we alternated between feeling sorry for him and want-ing to punt him down the nearest alley. His wife/nurse who seemed to function mostly as ballast ran around nervously trying to keep him upright and telling us over and over, "He's coming. Paulo's coming." Which after the first hour started to sound truly peculiar.

Eventually, we arrived at Dublin Castle. I am pas-sionate about castles, and medieval homes, really any old structure, especially made of stone, where people lived, and talked, and slept, and whispered, and spent years in affection or turmoil. I feel something physically when I'm there. It is a linked feeling to the people who lived their lives inside the walls. Yes, I'm aware that sounds creepy, but it makes me feel full and since Nan-cy and I were feeling rather empty these days I knew it was exactly what I needed.

Dublin Castle has one surviving medieval section: The Record Tower, built around 1228. It looked exactly how you would imagine: a tall circular stone tower with crenels and merlons that reminded me of a nine-year-old in need of braces. Nancy and I stood there telling ourselves we were not in Disneyland, but that this was real human history. Then our eyes drifted away from this stone evidence of long ago and we saw that what they call Dublin Castle is actually a complex of buildings, a hodge-podge of architectural splatterings designed by someone with multiple personality disorder. This is a site with an identity crisis: part fairytale, part Georgian courtyard, part business offices, part what-the-hell-is-that? It is structurally and visually incoherent. The medieval Tower connects with the neo-gothic Chapel Royal (also breathtaking), and then the complex veers off into a series of offices and it connects with four exceedingly odd square box buildings each completely painted one color from roof to ground: pomegranate red, powder blue, pea soup green, and Arm & Hammer laundry detergent yellow. They looked like huge tacky cereal boxes plopped into the middle of this otherwise moving historic visual. No attempt whatsoever had been made to create an aesthetic whole here, which damages the authenticity of the location and the emotional impact of the historical nature of the grounds.

In the ultimate dry understatement, Nancy rolled her eyes to me and broke our silence, "Might have a flow problem here."

"You think?"

Nancy was the person who taught me about "flow." She has exquisite taste in home furnishing and decoration, which came by her naturally. She was the person who showed me how to arrange my furniture so rooms flowed naturally from one to the next and it all worked. She knew how to create an entire living atmosphere. We stood staring at the peculiar buildings wondering who okayed this? Bert and Ernie? It felt a bit like painting a Speedo on the Statue of Liberty, or plunking down a huge modern glass triangle in front of the Louvre.

The Dublin Castle is, we learned, a castle sans crown jewels. The jewels were kept in a huge safe inside the castle office securely for 200 years. In 1907, while Sir Arthur Vicar was the Master at Arms, they disappeared. Scotland Yard was notified and they bounded into the investigation with their renowned Sherlockian abilities. They determined from the facts of the situation that the theft had been an inside job. They turned their magnifying glass on the castle's denizens, and oops, learned a little more than they wanted to know. Increasingly red-faced they found that the trail led to wild orgies and some kind of homosexual philandering involving Francis Shackleton, a member of Vicar's staff, (and the Antarctic explorer's brother) and relatives of the British Royal Family. In 1907 that meant hush it up, slam the door, pull down the shades, and shrug – which is precisely what they did. Interested folks who came along later, and tried to put the pieces together, found a number of key official documents on the case permanently misplaced. The whereabouts of the jewels remained a mystery, although many believe that Shackleton broke them up and sold them piecemeal.

From Dublin Castle we journeyed over to Temple Bar, a neighborhood named for Sir William Temple, a provost of Trinity College in the 1600s. Temple Bar sits on the bank of the Liffey River, which flows through the center of Dublin. This is a famous section of Dublin mentioned in all the travel guides to varying reviews. We were told it is a "must see" (which it was) and told it was a tourist trap (which it was). There's a reason why all those tourists are wandering around. This section of Dublin still has the narrow curving cobblestone medieval streets from yesteryear. It is packed with quaint eateries and numerous pubs screaming character and color. It is the central partying spot for tourists looking for nightlife in Dublin.

My son, Jeff, who spent a college semester abroad the previous year at Trinity College, had warned me that locals do not imbibe here. He insisted "Don't hang around Temple Bar late at night. It is full of pickpockets and vomiting drunks and is not safe." And there it was –*The Lion King's* "Circle of Life" staring me right in the face. So many times, when raising my kids, would I hear my mother's words come out of my mouth and it always surprised me, and then, it made me smile. How often do we think, "Wow, I sound just like my mother," and here were *my* words coming out of my son's mouth. "It's not safe," he said. It is a seminal moment when your child says something like this. His concern was so genuine, and so adult, I didn't know whether to thank him or shake him vigorously and demand to know what he'd done with my little boy. Remember the first time that flip happened and they cautioned you? Mom, you shouldn't go there, or do that, or drive there at night, or walk alone in the parking garage. It is new ground when the plates of motherhood make that tectonic shift. You feel proud and a bit curious. Who is this new person with these independent thoughts that sound so adult and whose nose I taught him how to blow just yesterday?

Nancy first felt this the day her son Matt did the over-under. He was in high school. Nancy went to hug him, and not only did she not need to reach down, surprisingly her arms were no longer above his. His arms were around her shoulders and her arms were now around his waist. The over-under. Who was bending now? She wondered sharply, *when did this happen?*

Walking around Temple Bar, I was happy to learn that Nancy was a strategic photographer, unlike Larry who takes a belt-and-suspenders approach and simply

shoots every single thing. He takes hundreds of photographs, which he never organizes or even looks at
again, at least so far, and we've been married 26 years.
He took over 20 hours of shaking video of our twins
when they were infants (and by that I mean blobs), with
them plopped into their little bouncy seats doing what
infants do, which is nothing, and the audio kept saying
,"There they are." And I told him dryly, "Yes, there they
are, that's where I left them." I admire his stamina.

Nancy said, "Hey, go stand under the Temple Bar
sign."

"Do I have to?"

"Yes. Stand right under the red."

Nancy was captured by the visuals and she was
talking about color and crooked light playing off the
skinny streets. I stopped and studied one of the older
buildings, put my palm on the stones, closed my eyes,
and tried to envision myself back in time, when horse-
power meant horses, when conversation was entertain-
ment, and when candles lit the world. With my eyes
closed I noticed the uneven curve of the stones under
my feet so different from the smooth characterless concrete paths we all walk now. And then, I heard a voice,
a tiny voice from far away, from the past. At first, it
sounded like a whisper, like a faerie's whisper, and then
it got a little louder. I could tell it was a woman's voice.
It grew louder still. I struggled to make out what it was
saying and then, yes, I heard it clearly. "Paulo is coming." Perfect. I looked down the road where Paulo and
Ballast were making their way toward the rest of our
little group.

Our Sandeman guide stopped us in front of The
Clarence Hotel and talked with more enthusiasm than
was attractive about the band U2. He told us that they
began right here in Temple Bar and that they told each

other if they were successful they would buy that hotel. And they did. The Clarence Hotel is owned by Bono and The Edge (that would be Paul Hewson and David Evans, respectively, yes, their mother's gave them names.) Our guide then waxed poetic, and at considerable length, about the band's music and career. And somewhere in the middle of his quirky history he launched into a description of the famous Octagon Bar inside The Clarence.

Nancy and I have never been consumers of the celebrity focused magazines; we genuinely did not care about what color lipstick Jennifer Aniston was wearing, or which newly fashionable third-world country some overpaid star was adopting a baby from (note to star: we have thousands of children right here in the U.S. who desperately need homes). Celebrities never captured our interest in that way, but celebrated places did. If a location had been the host to historic people, or events, that place interested us, and this was a very famous bar, and we were big fans of bars.

We stopped walking and looked at each other. Our guide was discussing in minute detail each of the 22 Grammys that U2 had garnered.

Nancy asked, "Well?"

"The Octagon Bar."

"Yup."

"We're not dragging around any kids."

"Or husbands with their completion complexes."

"So we actually do not have to finish this tour."

"We don't have to finish anything."

"Cocktail?"

"I'm in."

The Octagon Bar was perfect: the dome, the bar top, the leather armchairs. We rested our feet and enjoyed a cocktail in the midst of this visually remarkable setting and we began to feel a little special there. Children, husbands, parents we adored, homes, causes we cared about, and friends who relied on us, had created a lot of emotional clutter. It was not bad clutter (like what one finds on the throw out counter), but a level of ambient emotional energy that manifested as a sticky static in our lives. One of the consequences of all that life-noise was that it made personal reflection unattainable. There was so much emotional energy, creating so much life-noise, I had lost out on the kind of sitting around and pondering I did as a child, or as a teenager smoking weed in the woods. Maybe this was why my life with my kids passed by at the speed of light? Maybe it's important to stare into space sometimes – let your unconscious wander, think about things not related to any goal.

"The unexamined life is not worth living." I said aloud.

"Excuse me?" Nancy held up her hand. "I am halfway through a lovely gin and tonic and that sounds like a comment that will require me to be *all* the way through my lovely gin and tonic."

"Socrates is a two-drink minimum philosopher."

"It might interest you to know that Nicole's third grade art teacher, Mrs. Henkle, was a philosopher."

"Oh, is that right?" I said, picking up her teasing tone.

"Oh, yes," Nancy continued. "She carried this god-awful thick *History of Philosophy* book around with her, which I know she never opened. It was some kind of countermeasure to being seen as a third grade art teacher. Mrs. Henkle and I had issues, although she didn't know it."

"Oh, yeah? What?"

"Well, I'll confess, but don't tell anyone."

"Really? I'm in a bar in Ireland. Like I'm going to write a book?"

"Okay, so Nicole was in fourth grade. She had taken on this magazine drive for Muscular Dystrophy, and she was on a sports team after school, and she was spending a lot of time on her homework because her grades mattered almost too much to her. Somehow it got out of control."

"It happens."

"One night, she came in crying because she had math pages to finish and a little paragraph to write about her favorite animal and she'd just remembered she was supposed to do a self-portrait drawing for her art class. It was eight o'clock. The kid was exhausted." Nancy looked at me with that get-a-grip-smirk she'd perfected years ago. "It was a fourth grade art project and this little girl was completely strung-out."

"Oh, this is gonna be good."

"So, I told her, do her math and English, and I would do her little art portrait."

"I see." Now, I was grinning.

"Hey, we had to prioritize."

"I'm with you."

"And I did it."

"And?"

"And I got a C." My grin turned to a giggle. "Nicole was furious with me. And I couldn't believe it. C? What? It was really good. But what could I do? It's not like I could go in and say I'm an adult and it was clearly A work."

"Nope."

"C? I was so offended, and then, Nicole stomped around the house and taped it to the refrigerator with Mom and an arrow on it."

We were both smiling as the bartender poured us

another drink without asking.

"Hey, wait." I remembered. "Isn't Nicole majoring in art at college?"

"Why, yes she is."

And we both smiled and sipped. It was the most pleasant feeling to be sitting here, so far away, with no plans, in the middle of the afternoon, in the wrong time zone, getting a drink in this famous dazzling place with my little sister.

We started walking back to the Shelbourne. "You know, Nancy, I liked sitting up at the bar. We always take a table and I never realized how isolating that is."

"We get in the habit when we're dating because then you're struggling for privacy."

"Privacy is no longer a problem."

"Family home – no one in it."

"Exactly. I think when we go back we all should do more sitting up at the bar and ordering appetizers: several small plates concept. It is more social and the table's become a sort of enemy anyway."

The Monday night after we dropped Olivia off at college I decided to make a nice dinner for Larry and me. It had been rough going when my twins left for college and I had to start cooking for three instead of five, but I'd held it together so Olivia wouldn't see it and feel burdened before she left. I began setting the table with Larry at his usual middle spot and with me and Olivia on either side of him. It looked emptier, and felt lonely, but it was doable. It made sense. But that Monday night when Larry found me I was frozen. Dinner was ready on the stove. I was standing staring at the kitchen table (for I don't know how long) holding only two plates, two napkins, and two forks. No way. There was no way. The table looked endless and empty, and anywhere I thought to put the two plates down seemed wrong. If I put him at one end and me at the other end it was too far to feel normal. If we sat in the middle opposite each other it would feel like we were waiting for other people. If I put him at the head and me at he side I'd feel, well, off to the side. It was unbalanced and I felt the missing of those kids throughout my entire body.

"Hey?" Larry said tentatively when he found me paralyzed next to the unset dinner table. I just stared. "What's up?" He looked around confused for a moment, peered at the table, and then, he recognized the problem. It wasn't only me; he felt it, too. He stepped up, wrenched the table apart, removed the leaf, put it in the closet, and shoved the two ends of the table together. Carefully he took the two plates from me and set one at each end. We looked at each other, and we said nothing, because, yes, our world had shrunk. I knew that night that after I returned from this trip with Nancy things would be different between Larry and me. I wasn't sure how, but we had changed so much, lived through so much together. It was something I would have to think about and manage. There would most likely be dozens of little alterations in our lives.

Nancy and I were walking back toward the hotel and we turned down Grafton Street. Grafton is a pedestrian-only red brick stroll-way with shops and pubs and restaurants. There were a few street performers: a couple of really bad singers, and the usual guy painted head-to-toe in silver, standing inert on a box, basically asking for tips for doing absolutely nothing. We never got tips for doing absolutely everything, so we were disinclined.

As we walked along, "Wait a minute," Nancy said. "What's that?"

I looked. "It's a McDonalds. It's an attractive Mc-Donalds sandwiched in there, but still don't you hate it when you travel this far from home and bump into an iconic American example of bad-for-you food?"

"Not that. Look at the sign in the window." Nancy was exercised.

I looked. "What? Open 24 hours and...free Wi-Fi?"

"Don't you think it's a little puzzling that the mighty Shelbourne is charging us 20 euro a day, and even at that price, cannot figure out how to give two people in the same room Wi-Fi, but McDonalds two blocks away has it for everyone for free?"

"It does seem odd."

We crossed the pedestrian walkway and then we spotted Bewley's Café. Bewley's has a storied history, a stunning decor, *and* baked goods – a triple threat. James Joyce and Samuel Beckett both frequented this café and it was easy to see why. There were so many luscious pastry items piled in the window there was simply no walking past it. I defy you to walk past it!

Bewley's Café was built by Ernest Bewley in 1927, and with only one short retail time-out, it has been serving coffee, tea, and conversation to Dubliners and travelers ever since. We stepped inside and stood for a moment to look around. It was warm and stylish. It smelled like what I imagined Utopia would smell like: lightly browned buttery pastry, cinnamon, apples simmering in brown sugar, vanilla bean, ginger, pungent coffee, and mint tea. This was aroma you could taste. We walked past the piles of fresh bear claws and cinnamon rolls and approached the hostess who seated us.

The café had two levels. We were seated on the ground floor near six vibrant multicolored stained glass windows created by the Irish artist Harry Clarke. The ceilings were high and chandeliers hung low with a bendable pleasing light. The wood floors and mahogany trim were so dark and polished they looked wet.

"We should run from this place," Nancy said.

"Stop breathing in. We're gaining weight just sitting here," I replied. We ate there. (Truth: we ate there three times, because it was the most luscious blend of taste and place, and because the coffee lived up to its aroma, which I thought was impossible.)

"Nancy, try this coffee."

"I don't like hot drinks, you know that."

"But this. And the cream is silky and so good. God, I love good coffee." I held the cup with both hands.

"You enjoy that. What are you going to order?"

"I feel like breakfast. I was thinking about trying the organic porridge with fresh Irish honey and...sultanas."

"Sultana?"

"Yeah, I think the porridge comes with a concubine."

The waitress had approached and she explained, "Sultana is a kind of raisin."

"Damn, I was hoping for someone to do the laundry."

Nancy decided on lunch. I remembered that she had never been a breakfast eater. Lunch had always been, and still was, her preferred meal. She ordered the Tuscan tomato soup. It arrived a dazzling dark red color with flakes of basil, and drizzled with extra virgin olive oil. Chunky rustic bread had been cooked into the soup, and a hunk of it came on the side. Nancy tasted the soup, she closed her eyes and smiled to herself, and that little girl look on her face transported me back to our childhood kitchen.

When we were little girls, we trudged through the mudroom, into the house, and headed directly for our after-school snack. I always went for the Mallomars or Oreos. It was the obvious choice; the American way. Not Nancy. She would grab a tomato out of the refrigerator, sprinkle some salt, and eat it like an apple. Her devotion to tomatoes goes way back. The grown-up Nancy sat across from me now enjoying the ruby rich soup and all I could see was my little sister again, so cute with her long brown bangs and big glasses on her tiny face, swinging her feet under the table. It felt so long ago, and yet, there she was, again, with her tomatoes. Perhaps not so much had changed fundamentally – presentation, for sure, but the ingredients of us were the same. It was a warm surprise to have such a vivid memory of an everyday moment from our childhood together. I would never have remembered that if I hadn't been here with her right now. It felt really good seeing my little sister again. Maybe this trip won't only be about plotting a new future, but also about recalling our past.

When we left Bewley's we took a cheese Danish with us back to the hotel. Although we were too full to eat it, we were happy just looking at it in the hotel room. Then, we did a most outrageous thing, a thing a mother would never do, a thing we don't even want to admit to. It was decadent, unheard of, borderline unforgivable. We went back to the Shelbourne, crawled in between the luscious sheets, and we...yes, we turned on the TV. I know. In the middle of the day. We could imagine our sister Eileen rolling her eyes and sharing a judgmental look with our two husbands who were so much like her in temperament and energy level. Smothered in the Shelbourne beds, we were happy they weren't with us. They would not have enjoyed this galling downtime. The three of them would have been tapping their feet asking us what we were doing? Nancy and I loved this late afternoon respite so much we did it quite a few times along our travels and each time it felt decadent and astonishing.

We watched some smiley chick on *Animal Planet* try

to re-train some badly behaved canine. It was exactly like the few times we watched that *Nanny 911* television show, where some couple calls on a service to help them control their badly behaved children, and the whole time you think, *oh, yeah, they're terrible, I'm a much better parent than that.* Then, you go to bed feeling superior and accomplished until the next day when you get another call from the principal's office.

We lay in those beds for two hours between the cool yielding sheets and the down pillowed gentleness. It was an astonishing comfort. When did being in bed become so utilitarian? Get in, get out, move on, once a week rip everything off, wash and dry, and then begin the nail-breaking, enraging attempt to stretch the fitted sheet back over the mattress, where that last corner takes the strength of Atlas to slide over the mattress edge, and where sometimes it rips, and other times you have to heave up the heavy corner of the bed and rest it on your knee as you pull the sheet back on, and even with that it only goes on halfway, so it is not completely flat and you put the pillow over it and leave the room sweating and pissed. At the Shelbourne, an Irish faerie had made our beds while we were gone, and the sheets were crisp and the pillows plumped. The room was divine and we snuggled in and felt our muscles release and our jet-lagged brains sink into the feathers.

Getting into bed in the middle of the day was not something we would do, or even admit to wanting to do, in our mom lives. Could you imagine climbing into bed at four o'clock in the afternoon? At four o'clock you were prepping dinner, writing out the bills, or jamming the end of the broomstick down the garbage disposal in a harried attempt to dislodge whatever mistaken item had been shoved in there. My kids learned that the best way to deal with crisis situations of this nature (meaning where Mom was not an eyewitness) was for all three of them to stick together and claim innocence. No one pointed the finger at the other, which made determining blame with any certainty impossible. This created an all-for-one mentality, which we secretly approved of.

A number of times Larry and I were called to the grammar school by the counselor, who sat us both down, and used her syrupy tone of voice to inform us that there was a problem. Whenever one of our kids got into an altercation on the playground our other two kids would run over as back up and get involved. She complained that then she would have *all three* of our kids in the situation. We nodded thoughtfully, commiserated on how hard that must be for her, and then secretly high-fived our way out of her office. We approved of this family team solidarity – all for one, yup, that's us. So, while the counselor wagged her finger at us and warned that "Your kids should learn to fight their own battles," and while that sounded really good, we knew the world would give them copious of opportunities for that, and what mattered more to us as they grew up was the knowledge that they never stood alone while family was nearby.

NIGHTTIME IN DUBLIN

We purchased tickets to the Abbey Theatre before we left California. It was an historic place founded in 1903 by William Butler Yeats and Lady Augusta Gregory. There aren't many national theatres that can boast starting a riot, but the Abbey can. In 1907 it produced a play by JM Synge titled *The Playboy of the Western World*. The audience took offense at some of the language in the play, decided Irish women had been libeled, and tried to storm the stage. They were held off by a stagehand with an ax. Now that's drama.

We looked for tickets after we had made all of our reservations, so it wasn't a function of choosing a play, but just going to whatever was playing at this notable venue the night we were there. We found ourselves with great seats to *John Gabriel Borkman* by Henrik Ibsen, about which we knew not a damn thing, except Ibsen was a giant of a playwright, much admired and respected. Anyone who was anyone and was serious about the theatre knew Ibsen. He wrote: *Peer Gynt, A Doll's House, Hedda Gabler* – this was highbrow, sophisticated theatre (which is why I spelled it with an "re" instead of "er").

We had a very light dinner of salad and sandwiches that we picked up at Londis grocery and ate in our room, which was lovely; room service without the cost. Then, we set out toward the Abbey, walking through the early evening streets of Dublin. It was a splendid city night and we turned down Dawson Street to stop in at the Dawson Lounge on our way to the theatre. The Dawson Lounge is the smallest pub in Dublin, and perhaps the smallest pub in the world. It had been recommended to Nancy by a gentleman she met on the plane and so we decided to take a look. It was a bit tricky to find since it is only the size of a doorway, but we found it. A flight of steep stairs led down to the pub and we stepped in.

"Nance, there are no windows."

"No."

"Only one door."

"It's cute."

"It's a bomb shelter. How wide is this place?"

"I don't know, ten or twelve feet or so?" Nancy estimated.

"Someone thought it was a good idea to have a dark ceiling here? You know, give it that cozy you're-in-a-coffin feeling."

"Come on." And Nancy dove into the crowd of bodies and attempted to swim her way to the bar.

"Excuse me...ah, excuse me...ah, excuse me...sorry....right, aw...sorry."

I watched my little sister slap her hand down on the bar and say loudly, "A pint, please." I didn't know this Nancy.

The man standing next to me, or on top of, depending on your perspective said, "Ron's the best pour."

"The best poor what?" I asked.

"The best two-part pour. Ron pulls the best pint in

town." Is this a skill, I wondered? We watched the bartender. "It takes patience," the local continued. "Have to show some love to the Guinness, some respect."

"Respect the Guinness," Nancy confirmed.

"The official motto of Ireland," he grinned at her. (He needed dental work.) "Watch," he said to me, excited to have found someone who didn't know the details of this essential life skill. "First, you got to have the right shaped glass, clean, 20 ounce, room temp. Then, see, see how he's tipping the glass at exactly a 45 degree angle."

"Exactly 45," Nancy added. "That's right." I think the man was falling for her.

"There isn't an Irish lad from here to Shannon that isn't born knowing exactly what 45 degrees look like. It's in the soul. Then, you fill it three-quarters of the way full like he's doing, see that? And now, this is where the patience comes in, you have to let her sit. She needs to settle into herself like your ass in your favorite armchair." The bartender went on to other things. The local kept watch over our brew.

I glanced around again, "Isn't this a fire code violation?"

Some beefy curly-haired guy to my left yelled, "Hey, chief?"

A strong clear voice answered from a few feet away. "Yeah, Mike?"

"Lady, wants to know if this is a fire violation."

"Naw, we'll all throw our pints at it."

"Fire Chief says we'll all throw our pints."

"Okay," I smiled, "so as long as there's a plan, since evacuation seems like a pipe dream, with Orca hovering near the door there."

Mike looked over and saw the extremely fat man I was referring to. "Oh, you mean, Corky? Yeah, we call him Corky – always tellin' him not to stand near the door."

"Perfect."

We waited a long two minutes for the pint to settle and I felt the walls close in. Damn, it was tight in here. The bartender returned his attention to our pint and the local explained, "Yup, there you go, ready, see that, now he's toppin' it off with a creamy dome. In the wrist, you see, in the wrist."

The bartender slid the Guinness up in front of us and moved on. I looked at it. There was very little alluring about the contents of this glass. It looked not at all like the pretty golden delicious color of, say, a Corona. Instead, it was a burnt molasses color. I reached for it.

"Wait," the Dubliner nearly came off of his bar stool to stop me. "Not yet."

"Deborah, respect the Guinness there, girl," Nancy reprimanded.

"Sorry."

The local man eyed the glass like a stalking cat. We watched him watch the glass. Then, a minute or so later he nodded. "Now. And don't sip it. Only sissy's sip."

Nancy responded derisively, "Sip it? Ha!" And then she picked it up, tipped it back, and downed the entire 20 ounces. It was an epic move. That's when I had a fairly good idea of how this trip was going to go. She smacked the empty glass back down on the bar top. The local man bowed to her. A number of those around us mumbled their respectful approval. She turned and marched passed Corky and up the stairs.

Outside on the street, I was excited. "I can't believe you did that. How did it taste? It looked nasty."

"You know when you're cooking yams in the oven and one leaks and it drips down into the bottom and burns on, creating those little black pods?"

"Yeah?"

"Tasted like that."

"You're my hero."

"Hey, new things, right?'

"Absolutely."

She put her hand on her stomach. "I don't think I'll be eating for a while."

"No doubt."

We continued our walk to the Abbey Theatre. We passed the statue of Molly Malone, the life-sized, big busted young woman, pushing a wheelbarrow, presumably filled with cockles and mussels alive, alive oh. The locals call her "the tart with the cart."

The Abbey Theatre is not opulent like other national theatres. It isn't the least bit pretentious. It is rather small and has an ordinary kind of feeling to it. We located our two seats and settled in.

Nancy asked, "Is there a synopsis about the story in the playbill?"

"Not much. Says it's about a banker who falls from grace and how it destroys his family."

"Okay."

"I'm excited about this. I feel like I finally have time to engage with this kind of classic theatre and get involved, sort of an opportunity to grow a little, you know?"

We were ready to spend the evening letting this experience wash over us. We were out of our element, but that was what this trip was all about. Nancy said she felt smugly victorious sitting here a world away. During our average week, if we took a night out with our husbands, we went to the movies. We liked movies. We liked popcorn. It worked for us. On occasion we would go to a play, but rather rarely, because we don't have much in the way of worthwhile theater near us; if we did go, it was always a new production. Our theater history was lacking, the movies and television were where we enjoyed our storytelling. We knew we had ventured into an entirely new territory sitting inside the national theatre of Ireland, watching a play by the acclaimed Henrik Ibsen. We were primed and ready to be lifted out of the quotidian and into this new realm.

The stage lights raised, our fellow theatre-goers turned into seated silhouettes. On center stage was a living room. Around the outside edges of the set, a snow mimicking substance had been arranged and piled high. The scene appeared bright and frosty. Anticipation traveled like an invisible energy around the intimate, respected, Abbey Theatre. We were captured.

Now, I could tell you that it was a scintillating study of greed, jealousy, and isolation, but anyone would tell you that. What most theatre effetes won't share with you is that the first act felt about three weeks long. Nancy's knees were up against the seat in front of her and my ass was asleep. I had so many complaints about the logic, the inconsistencies, and the characterization, I wouldn't know where to begin. Yes, I just said that about Henrik Ibsen – true, at least, in this particular play. There were, however, two high points for us.

Nancy whispered, "Who is that?"

"Where?"

"In the lead, Borkman, I know that guy from somewhere. Check the playbill."

"Check the playbill? Are you kidding? I can't read anything anymore without direct sunlight or glasses. And I do think it's interesting that Mother Nature blurs our eyesight right about the time we start getting wrinkles and age spots. Pretty much the only kindness she bestows."

Shsssss...from somewhere. A few moments later...

"I know him from somewhere," Nancy whispered.

"He is so familiar. He's..."

"Umm. He's..."

And we both studied the actor, concentrating, trying to bring up who he was, which was a mental relief since the story and motivations on stage were so obvious and superficial they required no concentration.

And then, Nancy said triumphantly, a little too loudly, "It's Professor Snape!" Heads turned and I started to laugh. She was right. It was Professor Snape from Hogwarts. There was something smugly entertaining about this collision of worlds, which we really enjoyed. Now, we know that Alan Rickman is a really fine actor with years of dramatic credits, and I happen to like him particularly well, but we just couldn't help ourselves.

"Can't he fix this whole thing with his wand?"

"Why doesn't he just say patronus or something?" Giggle. Okay, it was juvenile, but it got us through the sluggish plot line and whiny characters. A few times I looked around at the audience and wondered, were people enthralled by this? Were they enthralled because they believed that if they were not enthralled then their neighbor might think them a philistine? Would their literati credentials be revoked? Surely the performances, especially Borkman's wife, were spectacular, but it was not enough to carry this turgid storyline.

I did say two high points. There were two moments during the play that hooked us. The first was Nancy's identification of Professor Snape, and the second came at the last climactic moment of the performance. Borkman was dead in the snow, and frankly, good riddance. The two women, who had become alienated from each other, because they had each had a relationship with him, stood over his frozen rigid body. There was a grave silence in the theatre at this final moment of the play. It was the pinnacle of this drama and it looked to finally deliver some genuine pathos. The two scorned women standing a few feet from each other staring at the body on the ground began (with painstaking slowness) to raise their arms toward each other. We can see they are going to join hands. It is their moment of dramatic reconciliation. After all the years, they are going to clasp hands in a physical and metaphoric reunion above Borkman's dead body. For the first time that evening, I was riveted to the action – the moment was compelling. With a tragic slowness, in the dark silence, their hands floated up toward each other, and as their fingers nearly met, it happened. In the absolute stillness of this emotional moment, in this packed theatre of utter silence, one extremely loud cell phone rang out! The entire audience gasped as one. Finally, we were all in emotional sync. Some poor man a few rows from us literally dove under his seat in wretched horror. It was a mind-boggling tribute to the professionalism of the actors that they kept in character and the curtain fell – the entire play destroyed. But, for as bad as that moment was, it was definitely Fate with a modern sound signaling that this play is over, really, so over.

It was about 11:00 p.m. when we started our stroll back to the Shelbourne.

"Okay, so if we ever make a bucket list we can check-off Abbey Theatre."

"Kind of an unexpected end," Nancy quipped.

"For all of us, especially the actors, but I like surprises," I said. "I think that was one of the things I liked most about raising my children, the unexpected, the surprising things they said or did."

"Yeah," Nancy grinned, remembering. "When Matt was four years old I took him out to lunch and all the way over in the car I was talking to him about honesty and how important it was to be honest and I could see he was listening. We sat down at the table at Ruby's Diner. This really sweet waitress came over with menus and said to him, 'Aren't you cute.' He looks at her and says, 'Boy are you fat!'"

"Oh, no. I could absolutely see little Matt saying that."

"FYI - there's no tip large enough for that," Nancy added.

"I wouldn't think so," I said. "Now, Olivia's kindergarten teacher, Mrs. Ross, takes her class to the dairy farm on a field trip and she told me during pick-up that the kids were all lined up listening to the farmer tell them about the animals, and at one point he says dramatically while pointing to the dairy cow, 'She can weigh 800 pounds,' and Olivia shouts out, 'Wow, that's *even more* than you, Mrs. Ross.'"

Nancy smiled and countered with, "Oh, yeah? Matt and I were standing in line at the drug store and Matt turned to the man standing behind us and said, 'Hey, why is your face black?'"

"How did that turn out?'

"Fortunately, the really nice Jamaican man had a sense of humor."

"One time I took Anna and Jeff to the pet store. They were a little loud, nothing unusual for two-year-olds. Some elderly cranky woman leaned down to Anna and said meanly, "Shsss!" Little Anna looked up at the woman, who had layered on copious amounts of eye make-up and dark rouge (as sometimes elderly ladies do). Anna pointed her finger at the woman and said really loudly, 'Clown!'"

It was only a 15-minute walk from the Abbey Theatre back to the Shelbourne, but it took us 40 minutes. Dublin, for all its daytime charm, is a nighttime town. We walked back across Eden Quay and headed for Grafton Street. We were more genuinely entertained by the convivial crowds than we were all evening inside the Abbey. People spilled cheerfully out of the pubs and onto the streets. Young couples kissed on corners and walked arm-in-arm. University students from Trinity College were arguing about politics on the street corner with a beer in their hands. It really does feel like a happy place. We saw a couple of drunken 20-somethings walk up to a local cop and slap him on the back and then they all joked around good-naturedly. We heard the smiling cop encourage them to find their way on home. We couldn't imagine that happening in the United States where the police are not seen as part of the community, but as an authority to avoid at all costs.

Once we had found our way back to the lobby of the Shelbourne, we stopped to speak to the concierge. Concierge – that's French for porter, doorkeeper, caretaker – you know, the smiley usually gender neutral person in the polyester suit sitting at the desk in the lobby. I'll admit I have a checkered history with the concierge community and it could be my fault. I have an inverse relationship with the Professional Smile: the wider it gets the more sarcastic I become. The Professional Smile has been perfected by the concierge community. Most of my interactions with them have consisted of getting restaurant reservations at places where I suppose they get a kickback, or trying to get cogent directions to some place they need to pull out a map to find. (I can do the map thing myself.) And asking a question always requires waiting in a line behind some yokel asking questions like, "Is it the same distance back to the airport? Do you serve breakfast in the morning? My stepbrother told me this hotel had beer from the tap, but in my room it's only water? Do I have to checkout at noon I was planning on staying two days?"

Well, all those concierge prejudices melted away when Nancy and I met Keith. Keith was a gentlemanly, bespectacled, youngish man, in a snappy suit, with a genuine smile and a desire to answer every question and be of comprehensive assistance. (NOTE TO SHELBOURNE: give Keith a raise.) He set us up the following evening for the famous Dublin Literary Pub Crawl, and gave us valuable info for the following day. And that was only the beginning of his assistance while we were there.

Before we went to bed, we got a chance to Skype with our kids. Skype is a gift. It turns a phone call into an actual/virtual visit. It is the best way to see and talk to your family and it's free. The face-to-face conversation is so much more rewarding than the voice over the telephone. The connection feels different, fuller; to see their smiles, and watch them roll their eyes when you ask if they're getting enough sleep. Skype was critical in serving our competing needs: to be connected, and also to be away. A disembodied voice on the other end of a telephone just couldn't accomplish this.

"The kids seem really happy," Nancy said. We were both in bed, lying on our backs, staring into the dark.

"Yeah."

"Remember when they were three years old?" Nancy asked wistfully.

"Yeah, tiny people all wild and emotional with their arms around you all the time."

She said softly, "That was the best part of my life."

"The best."

A tightness closed around both of our throats, like a little fist, because there was genuine loss, those little ones were gone – gone forever. We were mothers to these interesting, hilarious, lovely little creatures and they kept disappearing. The one-year-old gone, the three-year-old gone, then six, seven, seventeen – really gone. There was so much to love and to enjoy and it was painful to continuously lose them. There's a lot of letting go of what you love with motherhood. This fist in our throats right now is the sentimental acknowledgment that motherhood is a love designed to leave you lost.

"They were so fun when they were little."

"So fun."

"Night, Deborah."

"Night, Nancy."

We fell asleep drifting in the memory of those private moments that only a mom and her toddler share. It is usually a simple thing – an everyday moment where you are struck with a sudden clarity that it will all pass, and you burn it into your memory on purpose. Perhaps it was some homework project involving uncooked pasta that you both giggled over, or some costume where her head was the center of a big daisy, or that moment when your little boy fell asleep dog-tired on your chest, and he lay there all warm and slightly damp, and sunken into your body, his limbs heavy, and his breathing in sync with yours. And really only the mom has this memory, because the toddler doesn't remember any of these moments after they've grown. These are the privileged reminiscences for mom alone. Those moments that you don't talk about, but when you wish privately that they would never grow, never change, never be anything other than who they are at that exact moment. I was remembering a moment like that when I fell asleep.

A PHANTOM, THE LIBRARY & THE LIGHTNING ROUND

Very late, in the Shelbourne that night, I was awakened by the sound of a child crying. Where was it coming from? Was it in the next room? I couldn't imagine why someone wasn't comforting this child. Part of me felt compelled to jump up and help, the other part reminded me that it was not my child. Maybe it wasn't a child at all, maybe it was a whine from the elevators, or a cat? I lay awake for a really long time, and so, I learned later, did Nancy, since neither of us wanted to chance waking up the other.

The following morning, a bit bleary-eyed, we crossed to the charming Irish lassie at the front desk.

"Ah, excuse me?" I said.

"Good morning" she said cheerily.

I continued, "Good morning. I'm wondering, you know, last night, pretty much all night, there was a noise. It sounded like a crying child?"

"Oh, dear, did it wake you?"

"Yes."

"I'm so sorry."

"Did anyone check or call down?" Nancy asked.

"No."

"Sounded like it was coming from the hallway," I reported.

"It was most likely little Mary Masters."

"Didn't anyone help?" I asked.

"So hard to help Mary now that she's dead."

"Dead?"

"A ghost."

I said evenly, "You're telling us a ghost was crying in the hallway?"

"Oh, don't worry yourself a bit. She's harmless. She is just looking for her sister."

Now, I didn't want to be cynical, or insensitive, especially as a visitor in another country, but where does one go from here in this conversation? We stood for a moment looking at each other. The desk lady smiled with an expression that indicated all had been adequately explained, and then she asked...

"Brownie?" holding up the little pastry tray.

Nancy dropped her head and bit a grin.

"No, thank you," I replied.

Nancy asked, "You have a resident ghost?"

"Lots of people hear her. I never have. The hotel didn't know who it was for the longest time."

"And now you do?" Nancy asked.

"In 1965 the ghost hunter, Hans Holzer, stayed here with that famous medium, Sybil Leek."

Nancy repeated, "Hans and Sybil."

"Sounds like a puppet show," I said.

"Sybil was visited by this little girl at night, and the child said she was seven years old, her name was Mary Masters, and she died of a fever in 1791, probably cholera. So that would be before the hotel was built when it was just row houses here. People hear her walking the floors crying sometime."

"That is really interesting," Nancy said.

"Yes, isn't it?" the front desk lady said gaily.

I leaned in and said with as much gentility as I could muster, "I am just not that charming without any sleep, and my listening-to-crying-children-years literally just ended, so I don't care if it's a ghost, or a goblin, someone please give that kid some Benadryl so I can get some sleep."

Nancy forced a smile, took a brownie, and nudged me away, "Thanks." She looked at me and leaned in, "You're right. You're not that charming."

"One of the things I do not miss about motherhood is being woken up in the middle of the night. If by some freak chance of nature I've managed to fall asleep I'd like to enjoy it."

"Maybe it would be good to list what we don't miss about motherhood."

"Sounds therapeutic," I agreed. "So, number one: getting woken up in the middle of the night."

"Good morning, ladies," Keith-the-concierge said with genuine pleasure and then he helped us map out our day.

We headed out the hotel and walked over to Trinity College. The library there is renowned for its architectural beauty, and because it houses *The Book of Kells,* an illuminated manuscript created by Celtic monks circa 800. The manuscript contains parts of the New Testament and was housed at the Abbey of Kells in County Meath for a long period, and was given to Trinity in 1661 where it has remained. For me, this was a perfect storm: grand architecture, an old manuscript, and Celtic history.

We were early and so we waited in a neat line outside the library for the doors to open. It was a clear cool

October day. The students were all in class and so the campus was nearly silent. We read about some of the college's famous alumni: Samuel Beckett, Oscar Wilde, Jonathan Swift. When they opened the doors we filed in. Turning right we took a pair of headphones because we both really prefer the audio tour option where you can switch it off, or repeat something of interest. Now, I must have mentioned that Nancy is the techie in our family, and she can hold her own against any twenty-something these days, but even Nancy couldn't get these headphones to work properly. They were accurately sized for gnats, with buttons that worked infrequently or simply lied about their intent. We struggled and exchanged flabbergasted looks until we walked into The Long Hall, and then, nothing but the astonishing splendor mattered. I dare you to stand at one end of The Long Hall and feel worthy of that room. Here was a space that made me proud to be human. The Long Hall was 213 feet long, 42 feet wide, with 21 alcoves shelving hundreds of thousands of books, all the way up to the soaring barrel-vaulted ceiling. The wood for the stacks and for the ceiling was the warm brown of brandy. White marble busts of the famous lined the walkway. The long straight focus of the room with the books stacked floor to arched ceiling on either side of the aisle was mesmerizing. It felt as though all of the knowledge of the world was stacked up into infinity. A reverent tiptoeing of visitors kept the astoundingly gorgeous room in a hush. The blend of erudition, history, narrowing perspective, and the white marble statues against the rich browns; it was bold and soft at the same time - dazzling. This was exactly what a library would look like in a perfect world. I felt privileged to be standing there. Nancy and I smiled at each other. These were the moments when something new in our world startled us to stillness, these were the moments we were looking for. This existed and we didn't know it and now we're standing there.

After the library, we wandered around in the Irish sunshine and we did wonder where all the rain we'd heard so endlessly about was. We decided to try the Hop On Hop Off bus. The concept is you pay one price for the day and you can get off wherever you like and then hop back on the next bus. A number of these buses run in a tourist loop around city. Forty minutes and 400 why-I-hate-my-wife jokes later we hopped off for good. It was intolerable – how could any single bus driver know that many demeaning jokes and see fit to regale a busload of captive tourists with them? And didn't I-hate-my-wife jokes go out of style in 1950? We hopped off and saw we were in front of the Guinness Factory.

"Should we check it out?" I asked.

"Looks like a tourist trap."

"We are tourists, after all."

We ventured in, looked at the pictures on the wall, and learned that the brewery was founded in 1759 by Arthur Guinness. The building was leased to him for 45 Pounds a year for 9,000 years. Yes, it was a 9,000-year lease. We found out how much the tour cost, and admitted we didn't care that much about how beer was made and we headed back to the hotel.

I was excited about the Dublin Literary Pub Crawl that evening. Keith had booked it for us. Nancy was a bit leery.

"You don't think it'll be a couple of hours of dry bios on writers, do you?" asked Nancy, as we grabbed sweaters and were ready to go.

"It's supposed to be entertaining. And it can't be dry because..."

"We'll be in the pub."

"Several."

The tour started at The Duke, an historic pub open since 1822, situated just off Grafton Street and an easy walk from our perfectly situated hotel. A group of 15 assembled for that night's tour. Two professional actors began the evening with a little scene from *Waiting for Godot*. Then, they announced the plan. They would walk us around a bit of Dublin, stopping at a few pubs; they would do a little singing and some brief skits with anecdotes featuring the Dublin literary scene. At the end of the tour there would be a literary quiz and whoever won would get the t-shirt. The actor held up a black t-shirt with bright letters: Dublin's Literary Pub Crawl, and I fell for it. For whatever reason, that shirt had my name on it.

I looked at Nancy and whispered with surprising ferocity, "I want that t-shirt."

She grinned, "Um...okay."

"No, seriously, I'm gonna get that shirt."

I scoped out the competition – a varied group of challengers. I didn't know what I was up against, but I was committed. I wanted that t-shirt rather desperately. I'm certain there is a significant group of psychologists prepared to equate my feelings of motherly loss to a transference mechanism which drove me to want to collect this t-shirt. Yeah...whatever. The actors gathered us up and off we trudged to the first pub.

I happen to live in San Diego, only minutes from the border, so I immediately gave up on the Guinness pretense (since this was war) and switched to tequila shooters. Now, I was in my wheelhouse. The two actors eyebrows went up as I shot tequila at each pub while others were sipping their beers. Beer is just bulk and calories to me. Nancy was matching me drink-for-drink with some kind of vodka concoction called Sex On The

Beach – I'm just going to leave that there. I think she was missing Chip.

The actors were funny and charming, actually increasingly funny and charming. (Oh, tequila.) They performed little scenes and read from plays. Frankly, we loved the city walk and the entertaining monologues. And then we came to the end of the tour. Time for a quiz. I was steely-eyed or glassy-eyed – either way I had my game face on. We stood in front of the pub on Duke Street and questions were thrown out to see who could answer.

"Name two of the four Irish Nobel Prize winners?"

I yelled out, "Yeats and Heaney."

"Yes!" The actor confirmed.

Someone else yelled out, "Shaw and Beckett."

Damn, I thought. And it was on.

"Which Irish writer was imprisoned for indecency?"

"Oscar Wilde," I said. But someone else said it at the exact same time. We each got a point and we looked at each other. She seemed pleasant enough – undoubtedly some Masters of Fine Arts chick with an Australian accent. On another day I might have made friends, but like I said, I wanted that t-shirt. Everyone else dropped out and the Aussie chick and I went head-to-head for a couple more rounds. I could feel Nancy pulling for me. Finally, we were tied.

The actor said, "Lightning round. One question, the first one of you to answer correctly wins. Of these four Irish writers, which one played football, soccer to some of you?" (Soccer, what? I don't know anything about soccer. What does a literary quiz have to do with soccer?) "Was it," he paused for effect, "Fitzgerald, Beckett, Wilde, or Shaw."

I had no idea except I knew Fitzgerald was a ringer, because he's an American not an Irishman, so that left three: Shaw, Beckett, Wilde. The sassy Aussie chick yelled, "Shaw." I thought, damn, she knew it. The actor said "wrong." Everyone turned to me.

I calculated. Okay. It wasn't Fitzgerald. It wasn't Shaw. That leaves Wilde and Beckett. I eliminated Wilde since I knew enough about his life to guess he was probably not much of an athlete.

"Beckett," I yelled like I knew it.

"Correct." And he threw me the t-shirt.

"Whoo hoo." I was ecstatic or drunk or both. Nancy and I verily skipped back to the Shelbourne winners.

"How did you know that about Beckett?" Nancy asked. I saw absolutely zero reason to tell her it was a guess predicated on the process of elimination. After all, she was still my little sister and one never actually gets over that so I smiled knowingly and hoped she thought I was smart.

Back at the Shelbourne, I slipped in between the sheets wearing my new t-shirt.

"Comfy?" Nancy teased.

"Indescribably. I had to have this shirt."

She switched off the light and as we sank into the sisterly darkness she said, "You remember my girl-friend, Sharon?"

"Sort of."

"After her son Aaron joined the military she started collecting things. It began innocently enough. If we were at a party she would collect the used wrapping paper, and then she started collecting other things: teacups, refrigerator magnets, hair ties, and aluminum foil. We started talking to her about it. Really it was getting strange. You couldn't go anywhere with her that she didn't collect something. She just felt desperate to have things. To fill up that empty feeling maybe?"

There was a long pause in the darkness and I answered flatly.

"It's only *this* t-shirt, Nancy."

"Good, because if you turn into a hoarder I'm going to have you committed because that's just gross."

"Sisterly love."

"24/7."

WHICH WAY? WHICH LANE?

Two Broads hit the road. We were ready. Dublin is situated on the east of the island and Galway is directly west. You can drive across the entire waistline of the country in two and a half hours. Coming from the United States that is nothing short of miraculous. Where Nancy and I live you can drive two and a half hours due east and still be in the same state. Nancy had spoken to the car rental agency at length and she had us completely set-up; a small-ish car (so we could maneuver the narrow streets) a GPS, comprehensive maps, and an automatic transmission. Keith called to our room to say the car had been dropped off in front and all was ready.

In the lobby, we paid the bill at the Shelbourne. (It wasn't terrible at all since we were both basically getting a 50% discount by sharing – a benefit of *not* traveling with your husband.)

"Brownie?" The clerk lifted the plate at reception, and this time I took four.

While it was hard to say goodbye to the gracious loveliness of this hotel, I could not have been more excited since we were heading to my one and only priority: a genuine medieval castle. I had read *How The Irish Saved Civilization* and *The Mysteries of the Middle Ages,* both by the historian Thomas Cahill, as well as *A World Lit Only By Fire,* by William Manchester, and I felt informed and truly excited. I wanted to imagine, as best I could, what that world was like. Nancy had reservations about the quality of the mattresses and the functionality of the plumbing, but she was happy for me knowing it was a dream of mine. Her dream was also on the agenda, the Ballyknocken Cookery School.

We said goodbye to Keith, took the car keys, and rolled out suitcases. On the curb, waiting for us, was a medium-sized SUV.

"Oh, no, this isn't right," Nancy said.

"Nope."

"This isn't a small car."

"Definitely not."

"Can you manage this?" she asked me.

"Sure," I said. "Probably safer for us to be in something larger anyway since we're driving on the wrong side and could use the extra protection. The size won't bother me, in San Diego I've owned automobiles larger than some European cities."

"I guess that's right." Nancy was always smartly leery of my I-can-do-that attitude. After all, she knew me, and I can't say her apprehension was ill- founded.

We had decided back in the States that I would do all the driving. I prefer to drive anyway, and we thought it would be safer to have just one of us working that lifesaving learning curve. We threw in our luggage and then I climbed in and realized I was in the passenger seat. I got out walked around the car and got in to what definitely felt like the wrong side.

"Hold everything," Nancy said. "Where's the GPS?"

"I don't know. What does it look like?"

"It looks like it should be right there on the dash."

"Oh."

"We have to have a GPS. How are we supposed to know where we are?" She got out and walked over to Jiminy Cricket. "Where is the rental car agent?"

"He left right after he dropped off the car."

Nancy dialed the rental agency. I sat in the car and tried to get oriented noticing what Nancy had yet to notice that this was not an automatic transmission. The gearshift was on the left, which meant I would need to shift with my left hand. Hmmmmm...

Nancy got back in the car. "They said they don't have any GPS outfitted cars this afternoon."

"But we reserved one."

"I mentioned that."

"And?"

"And he suggested we use the excellent maps in the glove box." Nancy opened the compartment.

It was empty. No GPS and no maps.

She was back on the phone. "There isn't a single map in this car. Who rents a car without a map in it? Yes, we're still at the Shelbourne. Okay." They said they'd be right over.

I was okay with the delay, because I was staring at the road ahead and thinking carefully so if I'm turning left I would end up in the...let's see...the lane closer to the, let's see...

An hour later no one from the rental agency had come.

"Hi, Keith."

"I thought you ladies had left?"

"We have no map, no GPS, and the rental agency who claimed they were coming over haven't arrived."

"Traffic is very busy this time of day. Hard to get around. Might take a while."

I knew this was the case. I had actually planned to leave at the height of the traffic on purpose. I figured if we left then no one would be traveling very fast and I might have more time to figure out where the car was supposed to be with relationship to everyone else on the road.

Keith continued, "Could be a while longer still, but you know Galway is basically a straight line from here, you can't go wrong." He pulled out a simple one-page map and drew it for us. We thanked him and went back out to the curb.

"We're going to find real maps, right?" Nancy asked.

I reviewed Keith's scribble. "It looks pretty easy."

"You know what I was hoping for were maps made by map people, people whose job it is to make maps, those people."

"Okay, but let's at least get started toward Galway. We can stop at a gas station along the way for a real map."

Inside the car, Nancy put on her belt, yanked on it a few times to be sure, turned to me with her notorious directness and asked, "Deborah, can you do this?"

"Sure. " (maybe)

"I mean when you look ahead do you know where you're suppose to be, in which lane?"

"Course." (maybe)

"Do you think you can work that gearshift with your left hand while you're thinking about which lane and all?"

"Yup." Nope, not sure at all, but I saw no point in telling Nancy that since it wasn't as though we were going to turn around and go home. Why make her more nervous than she probably was already?

"We'll just go slow until I get the hang of it, and we're fine as long as we're going straight."

"It's an absolute certainty that at some point, and maybe some point soon, we will have to turn."

"Yeah, let's hope it's down the road a ways."

"We may also assume, since we are map-less, we're going to get lost," Nancy said.

"At least we have sustenance."

"A bottle of water and four brownies?"

"Works for me. Besides, this is like a mini-country, and it's an island. How lost can we truly get before we hit water?"

"True."

"Frankly, with the gearshift on the left, and with everyone else driving at me from the wrong direction, I think getting lost is not really our first concern."

"Perfect." She yanked on her seatbelt again.

"Ready?"

"Hit it."

We pulled away from the curb into the Dublin traffic going in the wrong direction with no GPS, no maps, and a vague intuition that west was that-a-way.

Truthfully, the first 30 minutes behind the wheel were the most intense moments of our trip (until the medieval tower incident). I could not remember when I had been so dynamically focused. As we approached the intersection for our first left turn I was working it through in my head. It was a higher level of attention than I have paid to any one thing in a long while. I kept repeating to myself your-instincts-are-wrong, your-instincts-are-wrong. Stay alongside the middle line. Keep the line on your side of the car.

"Deborah, do you know which lane? Deborah, here it comes?"

"Don't talk."

"Right."

"Left."

"Left. Right."

I think Nancy might have closed her eyes at that point. I was right about having the traffic, it was very helpful to follow other cars initially, and yes I might have heard a honk or two as we made our way out of Dublin, but ahead was the highway and it was divided and one-way so there was relief – we just needed to get there.

Once we hit the highway and started putting kilometers behind us a spirited sense of liberation settled on the both of us. We felt free and young and excited. There is nothing quite like driving into a new land, with no one waiting for you, no one requiring anything of you, and a full tank of gas. We were, indeed, accomplishing something new and we were already more interesting women – if only to each other.

Kilometers are deliciously rewarding for two reasons. Firstly, since 1 mile equals 1.6 kilometers, we were knocking off the kilometers fifty percent faster than miles even though our brain still calculated time in miles, which was sweet; and secondly, since the speed limit signs read 100 or 120 kph, we naturally felt like we were flying. The plan was to have lunch, spend the afternoon walking around Galway, and then head out to Clifden, about an hour further to the castle I'd booked. I intended to go everywhere I wasn't allowed in that castle. I intended to sneak down hallways in the dark, and open doors that were meant to stay shut, and climb to the merlons.

The Irish countryside, fertile and lush, spread out on either side of the road. Craggy remnants of fabled days appeared here and there as we drove; a solitary stone tower stood alone in a field, the remains of an ancient wall made of fitted rocks and dirt, strewn ruins unidentifiable except to say they had once been a part of something larger, something with a purpose. We watched in silence for a long time. These visual leftovers of an ancient past do not exist in the United States. It was a serene thrill to witness this material evidence of times we had only read about in books, and we spent a long time scanning the passing rolling landscape and realizing how truly different we felt, and what a gift we had given ourselves and each other. One of the comforts of traveling with your sister is not having to talk, and understanding when you shouldn't. Running away from home and vacating our nest-of-prior-purpose was the best choice we could have made.

"I was just remembering how I put the pots in the dishwasher."

"Most pots are dishwasher safe," Nancy replied as she scanned the countryside.

"No, I mean one night when they were all gone and it was just the two of us, I made dinner, put the dishes in the dishwasher, and even after an entire day I had room for the pots. With the kids home and all their friends in-and-out, there was never room in the dishwasher for the pots."

"That's actually a plus, right? Deborah, for our list."

"You know how much I love a list."

"I'll start," Nancy said, "You know your kids have left if...you have room for the pots in the dishwasher."

"You know your kids have left if there's gas in the car."

"You know your kids have left if you get to watch the Food Network any time you want."

"You know your kids have left if you don't need to close the door to the bathroom."

"You know your kids have left when the milk is sour instead of empty."

We approached Galway and that liberated feeling turned to agitation since the traffic became denser and my confidence in making the correct split-second driving decision disintegrated – not something I shared with Nancy.

"What does that mean?" Nancy asked.

"What?"

"That road sign: Calming Ahead?"

"Calming ahead?"

"What do you think that means? There is a calm. We should remain calm? Think it's like a rest stop in the U.S., for truckers?"

"Maybe it's a meditation site and we can pick up some aromatherapy."

"Calming ahead – does sound like really good advice."

"Words to live your life by."

There were quite a few cars around us now, most of them driving dreadfully fast, (the speed limit in Ireland, we learned, is more of a suggestion) and we were unsure of where we were going, and not completely confident which side of the road was correct.

"Wait, what is that?" I asked as we approached.

"I think it's a roundabout."

"We don't have roundabouts in San Diego, what do I do?"

"I don't know, slow down for starters."

I slowed and the honking began insistently behind me.

"There are cars all over my tail."

"You have to stop."

A horn blasted behind me. "Shit."

"You need to stop. You need to pull over." Alarm rang loudly in Nancy's voice.

"Where?" I asked, searching for an option that didn't exist.

There was nowhere and then a moment later we were in it. I cranked the wheel and tried to make sense of it.

"Okay. We can do this."

And we were in the circle. It was a tight roundabout consisting of a center island and six spokes leading out of the circle. Irish locals were buzzing around us like summer gnats, passing me, darting in front, angling right, and crossing my path.

"The inside. I need to get to the inside."

"Guy on the right!"

I swerved and barely missed another car. "I need to get all the way inside." I cut someone off. Horn! Craning my neck back and forth I maneuvered my way to the inside track. Nancy was pale.

"I can stay here, right?"

"I don't know."

We began to circle around once, and around twice, and around three times, and around... Other drivers entered, zigzagged halfway around or a quarter or more, and sped off onto their chosen spoke. We continued to go around and around.

"Which way?" I asked Nancy

"I don't know?"

"Okay, I'm going to focus on going around and staying on the inside rail here and you figure out where we exit. Then we'll figure out how we exit."

"Right."

This was when we confirmed two important things. Firstly, if you're on the very inside you can go around and around for eternity without having to make a directional decision and without being at immediate risk to yourself or anyone else; and secondly, that the Irish have an obsessive dysfunctional relationship with signs.

Each spoke had at least four town or road names on them and there were six spokes. Some of the signs were in Irish, some were in English, some were only pictures; it was chaotic.

"Go around again. I think we need that one, but go around again."

"No problem." I'd gotten the hang of the go-around. I felt like I was in a go-cart. I cranked the wheel and we whipped around the inside track of this roundabout probably eight times before we decided which spoke to take. Then, it took two more rounds or more for me to work my way to the outer circle safely and exit.

"Yay. Are we on the right side of the road?"

"I hope so."

"Are we pointed in the right direction?"

"I hope so."

"Cool."

As we traveled throughout Ireland we came to absolutely love the roundabouts. I would enter, maneuver to the inside track, hug the rail, and go around as many times as needed for Nancy to check all of the signs and make a relaxed navigational decision. We could have entire discussions about which direction and what the signs meant while circling. Not being forced to make an instantaneous decision at an intersection, and having this extra time to figure out which way we needed to go, meant we never took off in the wrong direction. It was dizzying, but nice.

GALWAY & PARKING IRISH

We followed the signs for Eyre Square knowing that was the center of Galway. As we gingerly drove into this crowded town we happened upon a sign that said Visitors Info. What luck?

"Let's park and go in there," Nancy said. I knew she was desperate for a map, made by map people, people who make maps, so we tried to find a way to park. So, now, let's see. The parking signs along the curb were nonsensical to us. How were we supposed to know what meant park and what meant don't park, fire zone, loading zone, who could tell?

"What do you think that yellow line along the curb means?"

"I don't know? There's a double yellow up there."

"Do you see a sign we can read anywhere?"

"No."

"Excuse me, sir?" Nancy popped her head out the opened car window. A smiling middle-aged man walked over.

"Yes? Glorious day, isn't it?"

"Yes, really beautiful."

"Can I help you?" He asked.

"Please. We don't know what the signs or those lines along the curb mean, may we park here?"

"Sure, don't fret the signs. Park anywhere you want, just put on your flashers."

"Really?"

"Sure."

"Oh. Okay, thanks."

"Where you from?"

"California."

"Beautiful there, too. Enjoy your day."

"Thanks.

Nancy turned to me, "Apparently the Irish take the same approach to parking signs that they take to speed limit signs."

"Think we should?"

"When in Rome."

"If we're in Rome we took a bad left at that last roundabout."

"There are benefits to being in a rental car in a foreign country."

"Exactly my thought."

I pulled the car to the curb, pressed on the flashers, and we headed for the visitors center.

In our time in Ireland, no matter whether it was with hotels, or other services, with people we met in the street, or with the guy next to us in the pub, we were enchanted by the easy friendliness and quick smile of the Irish. Except, yup, the visitors center.

"Hi," Nancy said politely, "I was looking for a couple of good road maps."

"Of what?" the woman said, never looking up from her book during their entire exchange.

"Of Ireland?"

"All of it?"

"Yes."

"Wall to your right."

Nancy and I shared a look. Nancy walked toward the wall of maps. I decided to question the lovely lady further.

"So, tell me, is this the visitors center?"

"Yeah." Still not raising her eyes from her book.

"Where a visitor might come for information and welcoming assistance?"

"Yeah." She sighed as though annoyed but did not look up.

"What do you recommend we see in Galway?"

"Wall on your left."

I looked over. There was another wall of brochures. "And where do the leprechauns live?"

That did it. She looked up. I looked back plainly.

"What?"

"The leprechauns. Where are they? Seriously, we haven't seen a single one since we got here."

Eyeing me and trying to place my tone, unsure she replied, "No leprechauns."

"No? Oh, how terribly disappointing. Nancy, did you hear? There aren't any leprechauns left."

"Tragic." Nancy said over her shoulder as she grabbed maps.

I asked the woman with heartbreaking sympathy in my tone, "So, how was it that they became extinct? Was it global warming? Or like the honeybee colony collapse?"

Now, I had her absolute attention. She was not swift enough to figure out I was playing with her, and yet she knew something was not genuine. She stared at me with her mouth slightly open. I held her eyes. If I could have brought up tears for the poor leprechauns I would have.

Nancy had a bunch of maps in her hands. "Let's go."

"Bye." I said and followed Nancy out. I could see the woman still staring as we passed by the storefront windows.

"Do you find it ironic," I asked Nancy, "that the only unfriendly person we've encountered in this entire country is the one person whose entire job it is to be friendly to us?"

Nancy's eyes were lit up. She looked downright gleeful.

"What?" I asked.

She grinned. "Great maps."

"You know you're rather easy to make happy."

"So true, although Chip may disagree."

We walked toward Eyre Square (pronounced "air" – like Jane Eyre). Close to the square is the Forster Court Hotel. It is a stylish place with a handsome bar and well located for what Galway has to offer. I used their restroom (okay, twice) and they were lovely about it.

We cut across Eyre Square and onto Shop Street. Shop Street – the street with all the shops on it. I suppose the street-name guy was tired that day. Galway seemed to have a way with the obvious. This was a pedestrian street with a dark brick walkway, which looked exactly how you'd hoped it would look. After a moment, a peculiar feeling settled in. It started with a free-floating suspicion and then clarity. We come from the land of television, film, and Disneyland; we know artificial turf when we see it. Sure, it was charming — but charming like a Hallmark card, with a vague kitsch aftertaste. The street was mainly populated by tourists, and the shops were meant to service their preconceptions.

"This is cute." I surveyed the street.

"Yeah."

"Why do I feel like I'm in Toon Town?"

"A little like Solvang," Nancy added.

"Exactly."

Solvang is a little town in Central California pretending to be a little town in Denmark. It has Dutch architecture and pastry shops. It's adorable but you never feel like it's real. It is more like being inside a life-sized dollhouse.

Nancy was committed to buying a Claddagh friendship ring for Nicole. It's a traditional ring with two hands and a heart. Standing in the middle of Shop Street there were a number of families claiming to be the original atelier. She chose one and bought the ring. We turned and headed away from the inauthentic crowd and were pleasantly surprised to hear two older gents sitting on a bench speaking Irish. Here on the western side of the island there are small pockets of residents who still speak Irish. (We were corrected by a local when we called it Gaelic – he assured us they call it Irish.) Irish is the official language of the Republic of Ireland, but besides the unintelligible road signs, this is one of the only places where you may hear it in conversation. The Brits did a pretty good job of stamping it out during their control over all of Ireland. The Irish government continues to make an effort to revive it.

We left Shop Street and wandered away. With only two short blocks between us and the shops the tourists evaporated and it was unexpectedly quiet. We took a right down Church Lane and walked alongside St. Nicholas Church. Up ahead we saw a very old stone plaque on the wall. It read:

This ancient memorial of the stern and unbending justice of the chief magistrate of this city James Lynch Fitz-Stephen, elected mayor 1493, who condemned and executed his own guilty son Walter on this spot.

It seems the mayor's son, Walter, racked with guilt,

confessed to murdering another man in a jealous rage over a woman he was courting. His father, the mayor and town judge, sentenced him to death.

"Irish tough love?"

Nancy replied, "A stickler for the rules."

"I'd say."

We just couldn't get our heads around this. Evidently 21-year-old Walter was beloved by his mother, sisters, and all the other townsfolk, many of whom begged and pleaded for mercy. Ultimately, not a single person in the town would carry-out the sentence. So, dad hung Walt from the window *himself*. (At which point, I'd venture to guess, that dear old dad never got laid again.) So, I ask you, is there anything that would make you physically capable of hanging your own child? Nancy and I stood there imaging that scene where he slipped the noose around his son's neck – how? Ugh. And a memorial to that event? Why? We walked away. Sickened.

Nancy said, "Our Grandma Kelly had an Irish tough love streak in her."

"Yeah, I recall so vividly one day I was visiting her in Long Island. I know I was young because my face didn't reach up to the sink. I said something that riled her and she actually dragged me to the bathroom and washed my mouth with a bar of Ivory soap. She scraped it all around my teeth, ugh, I tasted soap for a week."

"I don't remember her as well as you do," Nancy said. "I do remember once she told me my hair looked like a rat's nest. She said, "I thought you'd wanna know.""

"She was colorful."

As we rounded the corner we noticed another plaque, this one just to the left of a bright royal blue front door.

Nancy looked at me. "I don't know. Think we should read it?"

"I'm hardly over the last one."

"Let's hope for something less horrific."

It was a nice little notice indicating that this was the childhood home of Nora Barnacle, who became the wife of James Joyce. I am not a Joyce fan. I am not engaged by his prose, and yes, I realize that is tantamount to admitting to being a literary ignoramus, but there it is. In an attempt to understand this embarrassing literary failing a few years ago I read *Nora: The Real Life of Molly Bloom* by Brenda Maddox. I thought if I learned a little about the man it might give me a better road to accessing his work. Having read the details, the very personal details (really more bathroom details, and soiled underwear fetishes, than anyone needs to know) of Joyce's character and behavior, I gave myself permission to turn away for good. I found Maddox's book interesting and repellent simultaneously. Consequently, I had some really revolting facts to share with Nancy, who kept telling me to stop! But I am her big sister, and as already indicated, that relationship is immutable, so I didn't.

We decided to take a break for a quick snack of fish 'n chips, which we knew was a Galway specialty. The restaurant had a number of small tables, and one long picnic style table, along with an active take-out business. We slid into our seats, ordered, and noticed. Kids. Everywhere. The little darlings looked cute and we had a jolt of nostalgia. Then, hang on. Was it us or were these kids especially loud: complaining, whining, crying, even the laughing ones had an irritating pitch – just damn loud.

"What is that – a motorcycle?" I asked.

"That kid behind you has one of those deep bronchial things and is coughing all over the back of your shirt," Nancy explained.

"Awesome."

"I wouldn't drink that water, if I were you. He's spewing germs like a fire hose."

"You know, I feel a little odd admitting this, but I'm actually happy I'm not dealing with a cranky germy kid of my own at this moment."

"Truthfully, me too."

"This is nice," I said, "to sit here without having to mediate a fight, or wipe someone else's mouth."

"Or try to hide the disgusting drool on my shirt."

"Or cut up food."

"Or wipe up food."

"Or collect up food."

"Calming ahead."

"Calming ahead."

"Nice."

"Very."

Larry and I had a quirk about restaurants. It was a no tolerance situation for us; our kids were not allowed to misbehave in restaurants. It was one of the few places we stood firm. We never let our spawn run unbridled in eateries of any kind. It is not cute to have someone else's child in your face while you're eating. I cannot even count how many restaurants we abandoned in the middle of a meal when our kids were toddlers. If they got wild vocally or physically and we couldn't stop it we were out of there immediately. Those moms who sit blithely by as their offspring jump in their chairs, throw food to the floor, screech, or worse wretch, or worse crawl under your table, you know the moms who smile directly at you with that "Oh, isn't he precious" look in her eyes as the grubby-handed imp grabs fries from your plate – those moms make me crazy. What I'd like to say is, "No, your kid isn't that cute. Get your lazy ass up and take him out of here." Too harsh? In contrast, I genuinely sympathize with the mother who attempts to control her offspring and fails – those moms are easy to spot. They're the sweating, red-faced, apologetic looking moms who have run out of every conceivable bribe from Cheerios to chocolate in the hopes of actually getting to eat a real meal. These women are starving. I will, and I have, offered to help those moms in any possible way.

It was an interesting shift in perspective that came with the experience of being a mother, quite different from imagining yourself as a mother. I recall so clearly being in my teens and observing a mom in the supermarket with a screamer. The kid was having a complete mental collapse at the top of his lungs and all I could think of was, *why don't you take care of that poor child?* Then, after having kids, I can recall being in the exact same situation and all I could think was, *oh, that poor woman.*

READY TO HAVE FUN STORMIN' THE CASTLE

We found the rental car exactly where we left it with the flashers still on. Such an accommodating country. This would never have happened in Southern California. Private companies are contracted to run parking enforcement. They operate shielded by the authority of the city and behave like a motorized junta maliciously citing regular folk just trying to get a donut. They approach their job with a gusto that can only be called manic. And then they deny credible appeals with form letters. (A class action lawsuit has been filed against them in Los Angeles.) A few inadvertent parking miscalculations and they will boot your car and/or tow it away. It is not unheard of for strangers to throw their own money into the meters of fellow car owners if they see the meter running out and the enforcement guy at hand. We are all comrades in this struggle.

Nancy spread out her maps and directed me out of Galway. I was psyched about starting on our way to the castle – my one non-negotiable stop, and the highlight of my experience. I did have some concern about us driving any time near dark so I was pushing it a little. I wasn't ready for any new driving challenges. Nancy was so excited about reviewing all her new maps she missed a couple of driving glitches on the way out of town. I was grateful for that. Following her directions we found our way toward the Connemara coastline and Clifden.

It is possible that there are drives as beautiful as the one between Galway and Clifden, but it is not likely there are drives *more* beautiful: thatched cottages that looked like gingerbread houses, farmland so crisply green you feel it on your skin. This was what green smelled like, plump with moisture, with that elemental rich damp earth smell. Looking out the car windows at the moving lush panorama, so different from the desert-like conditions in Southern California, we felt like lucky to be visitors in this emerald world. Nancy and I relaxed and let the Irish world pass by us as the kilometers clicked along with gratifying speed. We felt settled into visitor mode. Being a visitor can be wonderful – or not.

The first time I traveled to visit my daughter, Anna, at her college, a thousand miles from her home, I stepped off the plane and hugged her fiercely. The moment my arms folded around her I had a relieved feeling as though something that had been dislocated was now reset in its proper place. I didn't want to embarrass her so I let go, but I could have held on for a really long time. She had borrowed a car from an upper-classman to pick me up. We walked to the airport parking lot and I got in the passenger seat. The passenger seat? That's different. We drove out of the lot and at the toll she had exactly the right amount of change ready. She took the correct turns and she drove me to where she lived along roads she knew and I had never seen. She pointed out the places she ate and told me stories about this or that event or evening as we passed. I was so proud of the way she had settled in. She introduced me to her roommates, people I did not know, and then took me for a walk around campus. Slowly I came to recognize that I was a visitor in my daughter's world. It wasn't that I felt emotionally separated because we were so tied, so close; it was that her life happened here, and then it was a story she told me later, as opposed to something we contemporaneously lived together. I could see how grown up she felt showing me around, and she would never have understood how pride and sadness were intermixing for me. Isn't that one of the fundamental truths of raising children — all those moments when pride and sadness mix, when experiencing something in the present is also evidence of moving on, like the end of the year school play, or that first girlfriend your son brings home? This visitor status was the proof that our lives had been severed in a fundamental way. She was showing me around her world. I told myself, she is happy. Look at her face. She is so excited to be on her own. I never told her how much I didn't want to be a visitor in her life, in her brother's life, in her little sister's life. I never told anyone how hard that sightseeing scenario was for me, or how I had to swallow tears the entire time. I smiled and told her how great it all was while I felt fake and empty. It was easier the second time, and then the third. Transition is harder for some moms than for others. I know it has nothing to do with depth of love or affection; perhaps it is more about the level of intimate everyday participation. I don't know. I only know it was hard for me, and I suspect, for Nancy, too.

As Nancy and I approached the western coast of Ireland, pools of water began to appear here and there. Large ponds of still dark water that came right up to the road's edge, and a fine white mist rose and drifted in cobwebbed limbs inches above the water's surface. It had a King Arthur, days of yore feeling. The road became narrower as we proceeded. In fact, it wasn't much of a road at all but was more like a glorified footpath for errant Druids and it added to that numinous mood.

"See those green mounds?" Nancy pointed, "That's where the faeries and wee folk live."

"Oh?" I smiled. "I was wondering where they were."

"The Irish do view the world magically. Irish folklore is loaded with spirits."

"There is an infectious mystical energy here."

"I am kind of sorry we learned the country is fresh out of leprechauns because I could really use a new pair of shoes."

"What is that?" I asked straining to see. "Ahead on the road?"

"Is it a dog?"

"It's pink."

"No, it's a sheep. Look, there's another one. Pink sheep? Maybe we really are in fairyland?"

"The colors are spectacular next to the green grass, the bushes, that murky water."

"Stop, I need to take some pictures."

"Take them from the window."

"Stop the car, Deborah."

"Do I have to?"

"Yes."

So I pulled off the road (which was tricky). We got out and approached one of the creatures wandering unfettered.

"Do they bite?" I asked.

"I don't think they care enough to bite."

Nancy couldn't have been more content snapping photographs and making comments about the angle of the light and the color contrast. I just could not get over half a pink sheep. Up close, we could see it was half, only one side was spray painted fuchsia.

Nancy said, "Probably different owners around here have different colors? Beats branding or tagging."

"The air smells so good. Solid and earthy."

"Like a dense moss."

"We're closer to the Atlantic and I can smell that, too." I noticed the sky beginning to look sullen. "We need to go." Getting back into the car I said, "I've waited my whole life to sleep in an authentic medieval castle."

"Sounds scratchy to me."

"Where's your imagination, Nancy?"

"It only functions on a good night's sleep. And I want to reiterate here that my idea of a good night's sleep involves a white sand beach, a glass of wine, softly rolling surf, and clean sheets."

"You're going to love this. Think about it – armored knights?"

"The poster child for an inflexible man."

"Ancient stonework?"

"There's a reason we invented insulation."

"Perhaps a secret passageway?"

"Inhabited by spiders and rats."

"Nancy!"

"I'm only pointing out that your view may be a tad romanticized."

The road narrowed and the speed limit sign read 120 km, which was clearly some road worker's attempt at humor, or maybe some kind of Celtic dare? I sort of like a good dare. Nancy gulped and said nothing, but I was aware she was gripping the door handle with nothing less than atomic force. As we flew along, there were times when I had to swing slightly right. I had to. I'm deathly afraid of water and it was right there! Right at the edge, on my side, where I was sitting.

I veered. A huge branch smacked the window near Nancy's face. "Ah!"

"Sorry."

Smack. "Hey!'

"Sorry."

Smack. "Deborah!"

"Sorry."

After half an hour of this, suddenly up ahead coming at us at great speed, was a committed (or committable) Irishman with one hand on the wheel and the other holding a beer. Maybe he wasn't holding a beer, maybe I just assumed he was drinking since who would approach another car head-on this way if sober? He was not slowing – at all. There was no geometric construction under which both cars could pass on the road simultaneously. Someone had to give.

"Deborah," Nancy said with growing alarm as he bore down on us.

"I don't know who has the right of way."

"Who cares! Pull over!"

"To the left, right?"

"Just Away! NOW!"

I yanked the wheel left, hit the dirt, skidded on the lip of the pond, pulled quickly back right to avoid a tree, swerved back up on the road, and came to a complete stop, where I shoved the car into park and we sat for about 15 seconds in silence.

"Shit," Nancy said quietly.

"I thought he'd give way *a little*." I was breathing heavily.

"He almost hit us. In fact I think he was aiming for us."

"Maybe there are rules about who should veer?"

"Our new rule is veer. We veer. I'm not up for playing

chicken with a wild-eyed Irishman."

"Agreed. Kind of thrilling though, huh?" I grinned.

"No. Not thrilling."

"A little?"

"No."

"Yeah. And when we talk to our husbands later if they ask about the driving thing we leave this part out."

"Definitely."

Warily, I put the car back in gear and we drove slowly up Sky Road (aptly named) to Abbeyglen Castle. We could see the turret and grey crenelated battlements rise up as we approached. We turned left into the driveway and parked. Sliding out of the car and into the countryside air I consider how many centuries wayfarers had been standing on that very spot, relieved to have arrived safely, having traveled long distances on horseback or on foot, having survived the highwaymen, the rain, and the harsh unknowns of travel in those medieval days. We grabbed our small bags and headed for the front. A bellman, overly elated to see us, scurried out to take our luggage.

(Now, before I go any further with this, I want to say in my defense, that I probably reviewed every castle in Ireland before picking Abbeyglen. I would venture to add that a mother facing the emotional empty nest transition, prepping two kids to return to college after the summer, and one leaving for the first time, and all three of them more than a thousand miles from home in different directions, dealing with the emotion and logistics of that, working part-time, taking care of a house, husband, and dog, and planning this runaway trip as well, perhaps that woman could get a little befuddled. I mean, that's understandable, isn't it?)

"Welcome to Abbeyglen Castle," the bellman said.

"Thanks," I said. "We're really excited to be....uh...

that portcullis doesn't look, you know, real?"

Nancy asked, "What's a portcullis?"

"It is the vertical dropping iron gate protecting the opening to the castle grounds."

The bellman grinned. "Nice replica, huh?"

"What? Is it cardboard?" Walking closer now I could see the walls, the merlons, and the turrets. "They're boards?"

He explained, "The house was built in 1832, but the medieval façade was carefully added in the last 30 years or so."

I stopped. Staggered. This is a set? Have I died and gone to Universal Studios? Who does this? Who adds a façade so a house will look like a castle in a land of *real* castles? Isn't that a little like putting up fake palm trees in Hawaii? Who calls their hotel a castle when it is certainly not a castle? I'm quite sure there is no definition of medieval castle that would include this structure. Who describes a castle in writing on their website as historic when it is not that old and nothing historic happened there? Who posts pictures on the web (I swear, *look* at the pictures) and it's all fake? Should I have known this? How could I have done so much research and been this screwed over? Am I a total idiot? Then, I heard it...

"Nancy! I cannot believe you're laughing."

"Oh, no, really, I'm sorry it's just that...well, it's funny."

"Funny?"

"That we flew six thousand miles to stay in a castle that is younger and more fake than Cinderella's castle at Disneyland an hour from my house."

"Americans?" the bellman confirmed brightly.

I was too stunned to talk. Nancy kindly took over the conversation as we walked up the steps and toward the front door.

"Yes, California." Nancy smiled. He was a typical good-looking twenty-something Irish kid.

"Surf's up." He said.

"Ah, yes, sometimes." Nancy smiled at him. I didn't have any smiles handy.

"Pass the taco sauce," he blurted out.

"Uh, huh."

"Dude. Where's my yoga mat?"

Nancy turned on him, "You'd better produce some faeries or they'll be trouble."

"Faeries?"

"Sure, this is Ireland, right? We want wee people and lots of 'em."

"Aw, there aren't any...oh, I get it. I get it. No taco sauce or surf, huh?"

"There is, of course, but California has 36 million people. It is the world's 8th largest economy. It is sophisticated and rural, desert and snowcapped mountains, so stereotypes simply don't apply."

"Oh, that's kinda cool – although the surf and taco sauce thing is cooler," he replied. "I want to start a business. A rags to riches thing. You know, the American dream, so next month I'm moving to Canada."

Nancy raised here eyebrows. "You want the American Dream, but in Canada."

"Exactly."

"Checking in?" The lady looked up as we approached the desk.

Nancy reached for her credit card.

I finally found my voice. "This isn't a castle," I blurted out to the woman who hadn't cracked a smile since puberty, which had clearly been unkind to her. I was feeling very cranky.

"Yes. Abbeyglen *Castle*," she said with a surly twinge.

"You can't just decide something is a castle," I said, flabbergasted. "A castle is a real thing. It's like deciding you're the Prince of Wales, can't do it – real thing."

There was a long pause and then the surly beady-eyed woman said, "Can we show you to your room?"

"You can show me to the castle."

"Deborah," Nancy leaned in, "we're here for the night. Let it go for now."

We took the room key and walked toward the room.

"This hallway floor is uneven," I complained.

"That's probably castle-like." Nancy was trying to cheer me up.

"It smells."

"Maybe that's Eau de castle?"

"It's bug spray."

The room was a suite. There was a large living room and a large bedroom. For any hotel room anywhere this was a lot of space. I tried to recover. I could hear my parents saying, "Anyone who goes on vacation and has a bad time is a dope." I tried to hold onto that thought as I took stock of the surroundings. At least these folks were consistent, whereas the pictures published on the Internet showed a medieval castle, which this wasn't, the pictures also showed elegant rooms with hardwood floors, sparkling windows, stunning furniture, a carved mantle fireplace, also – nope. I'm sure they had rooms like that – this wasn't one of them. I've stayed in all sorts of hotels and what really matters when I walk in is my expectation. If I'm expecting a budget place then I have no complaints. If I'm not, and I've paid for some-thing special, then I sort of expect something special. For instance, if the hotel called itself *a castle* I would sort of expect a castle. The upholstered furniture had that sour thrift shop flavor, the shiny fabric look than comes from too many asses in the seats. The threadbare carpet discouraged even the thought of bare feet. Nancy was making positive sounds, trying to lessen my disappointment, until she looked at the bed.

"Evidently the mattress is ancient, so that's consistent."

In all fairness the accommodation wasn't terrible at all. It simply wasn't the caliber of room displayed on the webpage. Our room was capacious and the view was verdant. There was ample furniture, even if it wasn't in a fresh condition. The room did elicit the suggestion of history, if not the actuality. I was fighting to recover when I stepped into the bathroom. The bathroom was early 1940s bachelor pad: an old tub with a round rubber stopper on a chain with one long yellow drip stain down from the spout. Next to it was one of those tiny pedestal sinks with the two faucets, one for cold and one for hot, a construction that never made any sense to me. There was no way to plug up the sink, and even if I could have, I doubt I would put my face in it, so washing consisted of turning on both faucets filling my cupped hands with half cold and then moving quickly to add hot to approximate warm and trying to splash it on my face before it dripped out of my hands. Naturally, this had to be done blind since your eyes are covered in soapy face wash. Next, I grabbed for what I decided to call an exfoliating towel (because I was trying to be upbeat). Most importantly though, if only I had known in advance about the hour lag time between toilet flushes then I would have been more circumspect on that activity.

Nancy was leaning over a little bookcase. "Here's a biography of Grace O'Malley the pirate queen. She was from this area. We should read this."

"Since we won't be exploring a medieval castle and so we'll have reading time?"

"Pretty cool, a pirate, chieftain, mother, and wife, who commanded her own army in the 16th century all along this shoreline."

"She probably had a *real* castle."

"Probably."

"With a genuine portcullis."

"Likely."

"And a drawbridge with a moat even."

"You are beginning to sound like a six-year-old. We will have other opportunities to see authentic places while in Ireland."

"I guess."

"Shake it off. There's Wi-Fi in the lobby. Let's go down and Skype our little girls before dinner."

The lobby sitting area was a big upgrade from our room, and when I looked around I rather liked it. It had a warm feeling. The place was growing on me. We settled into high-backed leather chairs, opened up our computers and logged into Skype.

Oh, Skype. Nothing like talking face-to-face. I sent an email to my daughter to see if she could log on. Nancy was able to connect immediately.

"Mom?" Nicole said.

"Hi," Nancy said, "we're at Abbeyglen (she whispered) *castle.*"

"*Mom*, you know how you told Dad while you were gone he was supposed to make sure everything was okay and check in with me?"

"Yeah?"

"Please tell him to stop calling!"

"What?"

"He's driving me crazy. He's calling every day. He's on me like white on rice."

Nancy laughed. "Oh, that's so cute."

"Not cute, Mom, annoying. Seriously annoying."

"Okay, I'll send him a message."

As we both settled into chatting with our daughters who were newly at college and were both effusive and full of news something odd began to happen. Bodies pooled up behind us. I kept my eyes on the screen, but I was aware of an increasing crowd breathing down the back of my neck. Finally, I couldn't stand it. I turned to look and elderly couples scattered as though they feared lasers might shoot out from my futuristic eyes. I could tell from their gawking faces they had never seen Skype, were alarmed by the disembodied face of my daughter, and were wondering why the TV-like screen was talking to me. I thought this was a techie country, but I'm guessing from the crowd that half of these people didn't even own computers. I opened my mouth to explain, but they scurried away spooked. Nancy and I said goodbye to our girls and faced each other. We had each noticed two important things about that crowd of guests. Firstly, we may be the only guests in this hotel under 75 years old; and secondly, they were dressed for dinner. No, I mean *dressed*. We're talking gowns.

My sister asked pointedly, "Did you see what they're wearing?"

"Strange."

"Let's review. Which one of us insisted on bringing no good clothes whatsoever and only one small suitcase? I remember she said to me, 'Why would we ever need anything fancy? Or even anything mildly nice?' Hummmmm, who was that again?"

"Look, I had no way of knowing we were going to wind-up in this fake castle with the cast from the Retirement Home for the Overly Dressed."

"One of us speculated that we might not know what we would need and so should bring a real suitcase and be prepared, and the other one of us was adamant about us not needing anything but jeans."

"Yes, well, I may have been wrong about that," I said.

"May have been?"

"Waiting for it...waiting for it..."

"I told you so."

"Perfect. Feel better?"

"Surprisingly, yes. We have to eat, and there is nowhere else, so all we can do is change into our clean jeans and our nicest shirt."

"Right. It'll be fine."

We were getting up from our comfy leather chairs when it happened –when he happened – the proprietor Paul. Paul blew into the lobby with the personal force of an F5 twister and the bubbly cheer of Dory from *Finding Nemo*. An eccentric innkeeper with an infectious grin and a gregarious presence, of all the characters we met along our trip, Paul Hughes was our favorite. He approached and greeted us as though he'd been waiting for us to arrive for years, like we had located his lost dog, like we carried the key to his immortality. Although we guessed him to be in his sixties, Paul had the amiable buoyancy of a nine-year-old boy. He was wearing a colorful suit and his extravagant welcome was warm and utterly genuine. I have never been welcomed into a hotel this way. I bet returning soldiers haven't been welcomed into their own homes with this much enthusiasm. One time the Doubletree Inn gave me a warm cookie (and I do love a warm cookie), but really that was kids stuff compared to this.

We learned that Abbeyglen was originally built as a hunting lodge, fell into disrepair when money got tight, and functioned as an orphanage in the 1950s. The Hughes family purchased it in 1969 and they've been here ever since. Paul encouraged us to get ready for dinner. We must be hungry. We were. We didn't have the heart to tell him that our 'getting ready' was going to be a disappointment for him.

We changed into our least worst shirt and our cleanest jeans and headed for the dining room. Everyone was already seated. It had a little bit of a cruise ship feeling: everyone eating at the same time, older crowd, people who had spent some serious waking hours pulling together their outfits, women who understood accessories, which I never have. It was a huge dining room with crisp white tablecloths and pristine wine glasses shimmering in candlelight. The tables were stunningly set and the effect was elegant. The room smelled of spices and of roasted garlic and caramelizing onions.

We stepped in and Paul flew over to lead us to our table. If there were a dining room dress code he graciously never let on. He sat us at a lovely table for two on which Paul had put a little American flag and a Polaroid picture of the two of us arriving. Seriously, this may be the cutest man on the planet. Our impression of Abbeyglen was shifting so fast we needed to bend our knees for balance.

There were a number of menu options. Regrettably, it was pricey for us, so we decided to order a la carte a main dish each and forego the appetizers and desserts. We noticed another table for two with a little Norwegian flag on it and the only young couple in the room. They were gazing into each other's eyes. They were nicely dressed, but not in formal wear since she was about six months pregnant.

Those few months in the middle of the pregnancy were generally the best. During the first three, there was the vomiting, irritability, and insomnia. The last two months, there was the relentless pressure, the itching, the fear, the backache, the peeing, and the swelling. Yup, I would say months four, five, and six were the gazing into each other's eyes time.

That seemed so long ago, those beginning moments of building a family together. The hours you spend trying to choose the name that will follow your child forever. Finding out that all of your favorite names are off the list because they are names of your husbands' ex-girlfriends or a relative he can't stand. Nixing his names because they sound oddly ethnic, or clunky, or have too many syllables. The entire time feeling how terribly crucial it is to get the name right. With your first child, of course, you haven't yet learned how smart it is to keep this debate solely between the two of you. Decide and then make an announcement as a done deal. Most often young parents mention their considerations to their parents, their in-laws, their siblings, and then you really go crazy as every single person has an opinion and usually a visceral reaction. Suddenly the name of your baby is everyone's job. This is when you do not remember, but your sister reminds you, that when you were eight-years-old she *told* you she was going to name her little girl Elizabeth and so you can't. She says petulantly, "I called it." And you are eight again because with your sisters you are always little kids inside.

We had no idea what to expect in the way of food at Abbeyglen, since I hadn't paid attention to that element at all when I booked the reservation since I was there for the medieval history and...oh, never mind.

We were pleasantly startled when Paul pulled up a chair, plopped right down, and joined us at our table. He spent a few minutes chatting with us and then just as smoothly moved on to another guest.

Nancy said, "Maybe *he's* the leprechaun."

"He's cheerful enough. They are supposed to be cheerful, right?" I asked.

"I only know the one on the Lucky Charms box and

he seems cheerful enough."

So far everything about Abbeyglen had been unpre-dictable and remarkable. And that continued. Dinner arrived. I ordered a mushroom pasta pesto and Nancy ordered some kind of fancy chicken dish.

You know that first bite of something when it sits on your tongue and you pause reflexively as your taste buds conduct the hallelujah chorus in your mouth? Confession: I am the opposite of a foodie (in fact the things I will not eat, and the reasons I will not eat them, are so lengthy and complex I need an excel spreadsheet to explain it to myself). But this. This required no food-ie credentials, because this was bliss on a fork. People always consider that someone deeply committed to food and wine, folks who go to tasting festivals, own 40 cook-books, and know chefs by their first names, are the peo-ple to impress. Not so, I'd argue. Try to impress me – a person who couldn't care less about food and would be happy if we could substitute vitamins and just get on with our day – making me care is an accomplishment. We hadn't expected anything in the way of an exception-al meal until we arrived at Nancy's one non-negotiable stop: the cooking school in Ballyknocken. I looked up from my plate and into Nancy's eyes. Nancy has a little of the connoisseur in her. She happens to be a wonder-ful cook and if you go to a dinner party at her house you should expect the fancy dishes, the good glasses, and those ringy things that put a choke hold on the cloth dinner napkins.

Nancy was staring at her plate.

"Nancy?"

"Oh, my."

"Me, too."

"Taste this."

We shared bites and then ate in silence, smiling now

and then. It was a shame we couldn't have sampled the appetizers and desserts, but we were so full we couldn't have eaten it anyway. This was the best meal we had in Ireland. We had traveled so far for this "castle," and found instead the real reason everyone was here was the food.

Paul insisted we go into the bar after dinner for a drink and some music. We crossed into the small lounge where there were several tables, a long lovely bench booth, and some bar stools. The fireplace added warmth and there was a young man providing live music. Remembering our conversation in the Octagon Bar back in Dublin, we opted for the bar stools. I ordered a tequila, straight up, very cold, and was given a Baileys. Nancy ordered a vodka, soda, olive, and was given a Baileys. Gotta love this place.

Well-fed we sank into the ambiance of this special lounge. While getting to know the bartender, and telling her about our trip, two gentlemen came up behind us. They were gristly guys, one had a stringy comb-over – the other had a cane. It was a self-redefining moment. These two men were, how shall I put this gracefully... codgers? They put their arms around our shoulders and jovially engaged in some light banter, privileging us with a close-up view of their over-sized dentures that clicked as they spoke. Oh, dear. Is this who we are now? Is this what the net of our womanly charms catches? We put on our most sincere expressions, laughed with them, finished our Baileys, excused ourselves and headed back to our room.

Nancy whispered along the way, "Have you noticed that the quality of men now hitting on us has seriously deteriorated?"

"I didn't know whether to give them our phone number or CPR."

"There really should be an expiration date on that kind of behavior."

"If you cannot touch your knees or remember your middle name, really, it's time to give it up."

We do not see ourselves honestly. I realize that. I look in the mirror and I still see the 30-year-old I was (if the lights are low). That is why I'm always so stunned in family pictures. Who is that? Neither Nancy nor I have had any Botox or lifts or peels or anything else yet. I can't say we never will, because who knows what's ahead. We have good genes. From my other girlfriends, though, I understand that it is not so much about looking like a youngster as it is about finding yourself again underneath the wrinkles, cottage cheese thighs, and sagging chin lines. Many times it's a function of not recognizing, not accepting the face in the mirror as you. How much better we look in the mirror through the soft focus of aging eyes. There are many positive changes of growing older, but managing the flirtatious fantasies of two guys with a few too many miles on them was not one of them.

Back in the room, we crawled into bed and thought about our evening.

I said quietly, "You know I got it. It came in the mail."

"What?"

"It...the AARP card."

"No."

"Yes."

"Holy shit."

"No kidding."

"How rude," Nancy snapped, "it's not time yet."

"Felt like a slap in the face."

"What did you do?" Nancy asked.

"Swore out loud and dropped it in the trash like it was radioactive."

"I understand. I'm not ready."

"Me, either." I said.

"Do you think we're still attractive to our husbands?"

"I hope so. I mean, I don't waltz around the bedroom naked anymore like I used to when we first married. I think a little subterfuge by the way of attractive nighties and light make-up provide a necessary camouflage, but I'm not sure if I'm doing it for my sake or for his."

"I try not to look in a full-length mirror."

"My bathing suit days are over," I admitted.

"Yeah, I bought a number of cute cover-ups and I use those when I'm not actually underwater. Gravity's a bitch."

"Having children did force a bodily redistribution I'm not that fond of, but it's the passing years that have really loosened things up around the edges. Sucks."

"So sucks," Nancy agreed.

"Should we care?"

"I think it's healthy to care."

"I feel better when I look good; I know that. I do judge harshly other middle-aged people who don't care, who walk around sloppy and gushy in too tight stretch pants and crocs. So, I suppose I do it for myself; it's how I'm comfortable."

"It was fun talking to the bartender about our travels," Nancy said. "Made me feel interesting. "

"Being parents makes people boring."

"Deborah, that's ridiculous. It adds hugely to your life. It adds perspective and life experience. I've found people without children can be much more boring and self-absorbed."

"But over the last 20 years conversations about my kids, or someone else's kids, have dominated nearly every exchange. Even when I'm out with another couple and I actively try to change the subject it reverts back. It's boring."

"True. Same thing happens to us when we're out."

I complained. "After a five-minute catch-up on what everyone's kids are doing I would rather talk about current events, or vacation trips, or books, or movies, or history. It feels though like kid-talk is the only safe common ground."

"Maybe we need new friends." Nancy smiled.

"Maybe they feel exactly the same way."

"And maybe this is actually what this trip is all about: changing the conversation."

"I'm in."

LOOKING FOR LOVE IN LISDOONVARNA

We were up by dawn and out of the hotel in a flash. The bed was sub-standard and the bathroom not worth using. Still, Abbeyglen was a lot like that favorite dog you had – the one who peed in the wrong place and chewed the wrong things – the dog whose saliva you swabbed to get that DNA test to learn she wasn't at all what you expected, and still you loved her and wouldn't change her for the world. Abbeyglen the Almost Castle actually was a highlight, albeit in unexpected ways. We did feel a wee bit like we were sneaking out since we didn't want to run into Paul while escaping this early in the morning. Hurting his feelings in any way was out of the question for us. I took the front steps, two at a time, and Nancy stopped me.

"Wait," Nancy whispered. "You have to take a picture of me at the front door." She stood next to the door, crossed her legs, and cocked her head.

I quickly snapped the shot on her camera and we loaded into the car.

"You wanted a picture of you like that in the front of

the Shelbourne, too. What's with you and the front door pictures?" I asked.

"For Nicole's first day of kindergarten, I took a picture of her standing at our front door with her lunch box and pony tail. She'd crossed her skinny legs and cocked her head. She was so nervous and shy. She appeared tiny up against the big door. Then, every year after that, for the first day of school I had her stand in the same spot, in the exact same pose, and I took the same photo."

"How'd that go over when she hit high school?"

"There may have been a little attitude. But I got that in the picture, too, which was great. I have a photo album of her year after year standing exactly like that in front of our door for her first day of school – all the way through 12th grade. So, a couple of weeks ago..." I could hear Nancy's throat constrict just a tiny bit. "I went out to our mailbox and there was a letter from Nicole. I opened it. It was just one picture. She was standing, her legs crossed, her head cocked, in front of the door to her dorm, ready for her first day at college." Both of our eyes welled up. "She had her roommate take the picture and she sent I to me."

"Oh, that was sweet of her. How hard did you cry?" I asked.

"Pretty hard."

"Yeah, those memory tears are painful."

"I emailed Nicole that photo you took of me outside Shelbourne and now I'll email this one too."

"Very cool, Nancy."

"Yeah. And every place we stay."

"Yes." We drove away.

We were heading for the cliff – the Cliffs of Moher (pronounced more). We drove down the west coast cautiously since the road was a sidewalk with an occasional errant fuchsia sheep, and at other times a sheer drop off the side.

Nancy and I had changed. There was a palpable shift in our core. We were in no hurry - genuinely. We weren't just telling ourselves we were in no hurry – we had honestly achieved an unhurried state. There were no lists running in the back of my mind. Last night, we crossed some new kind of personal time zone. The hurrying that had driven every moment of every day for so many years simply ended. It wasn't that we were telling each other we had no pressure to be anywhere, we truly felt no pressure. Something had let go inside and a sense of whenever-whatever took its place. It didn't matter how long it took us to get to the Cliffs – whatever.

"Nancy, remember those family vacations when the kids were little, where we were always looking for a quiet summer spot to relax, as though it were *about* the spot."

"The only thing more work than a regular day with little kids was taking them on vacation."

"Yeah, the vacations were killers," I said. "Like giving birth. If we remembered with any accuracy how much it hurt, then no woman would ever have more than one child, but nature makes us forget. I think vacations are like that when the kids are little. Every year you're under the impression that you're going on a vacation, and then you get there and the workload is worse than being home. Instead of a hotel, we'd always look for a condo or apartment to keep the costs down. That way we wouldn't have to eat out every meal, not really focusing on the fact that I would then be shopping and cooking."

"And all the washing and packing and games to keep them occupied while traveling," Nancy added.

"And a vacation is usually by water – a lake, an ocean – so there's the added thrill of watching like a hawk that no one drowns."

Nancy said, "The last place a mom can relax is on vacation with her kids."

"Right now is the most relaxed I can ever remember feeling."

"Calming ahead."

"Calming ahead."

Just when we thought this country couldn't get any cuter we pulled into Lisdoonvarna, a quaint village of about 900 residents in County Clare along the way to the Cliffs of Moher. The main street has the typical line of colorful storefronts and restaurants. It was what we had come to expect from a little Irish town. We weren't expecting much in the way of a surprise and then – the sign "Lisdoonvarna Home of the Matchmaking Festival – Europe's Biggest Singles Event."

"They're kidding. This place?" Nancy asked wide-eyed.

Eleven months out of the year this is a sedate little village. Then for the entire month of September, this town swells to 40,000, swarming with bachelors and bachelorettes come to market themselves. Farmers, fishermen, lorry drivers, locals, along with observing tourists, all flock in with romantic hopes for a solid month of dancing, drinking and professional matchmaking. Yes, professional matchmaking. We were amused. We couldn't imagine what September would be like in this hamlet. And, yes, we both understood the irony of we two Americans finding this amusing, since we traveled here from a country that finds marriage partners on TV shows.

The official matchmaker is Willie Daly, who inherited the role. He is a fourth generation matchmaker and he hangs out at The Matchmaker Bar in the center of town. The romantic hopefuls fill out an application with Willie and he uses it to match folks up. Dancing goes on most of the day and all night long to live music. Evidently, people of all ages and sizes and backgrounds travel here from all over (including the U.S.) looking for love. It is the oldest, largest, matchmaking festival on the planet. I'm really sorry we didn't arrive a month earlier so we could have seen it, but we didn't know. We did go into the bar and look around. There were pictures of the event all over town. It was sublimely tacky. What was absorbing about it was they all looked like real people. A little worn, maybe a little doughy, but so happy spinning on the dance floor, laughing in their beers. We were told there were couples who met here and then returned year after year to celebrate it as an anniversary. Some have been returning for over 50 years. Looking for love in all the wrong places? Check out Lisdoonvarna. Ireland continued to surprise us.

Perhaps that's what we're craving – the confirmation that there were still surprises ahead for us even though our kids were gone and our lives changed. Having children is a world of continuous surprises. You're surprised when they take their first step, when they use their first compound verb, when you find out they are good at a sport, or an instrument, or they got a part in the school play. It was all delightfully surprising – the way kids see the world – the things they say. Some of those things stick with you forever and still make you smile years later.

One fall evening, I was driving along the Pacific Coast Highway and my four-year-old, Anna, was watching the sun dip closer and closer to the ocean water. It was a rare peaceful moment. We were coming back from a kid art school where they drew over your child's own work and then presented it to you as though your child had drawn it unassisted, and so until you caught on, you thought you were raising Georgia O'Keefe and you kept buying classes. (Still a little bitter about that.) We were watching the sun set.

"Mommy?"

"Yes?"

"When the sun goes down into the ocean is it daytime for the fishes?"

Following her gaze to the horizon and seeing the sun dip in at the edge of the water, well, it was a perfectly sensible question. This was, however, the same child who, when she was in middle school and we had an electrical outage, stormed into the kitchen and said, "Mom, can you *please* get the electricity fixed because I really need to flush the toilet." Not too quick on the home repair front. Although her sister could match her on auto repair. Olivia, at about the same age, accompanied me to Discount Tire.

Tire Man said, "The other tires look pretty good."

"Okay." I was happy.

"We'll fix the leak in the spare and put it back."

"Great," I said.

"We probably need to rotate the tires."

"Oh, c'mon?" Olivia interrupted like she'd trapped him now! "The tires *already* rotate."

He smiled uncertainly and looked at me. I bit the sides of my grin to keep from laughing out loud.

Sometimes they said things over and over and I had no idea what it meant so I'd just carry on. When Anna was little enough to still be in a highchair, and I was running around making dinner, she would look up suddenly, scared, and say with the hope of confirmation, "No. There's *no* chicken outside?"

I thought maybe it had something to do with the Big Bird movie. I would reassure her, "No, honey, there's no chicken outside." This happened for months a couple of nights a week. She would look up suddenly and say in her little girl voice with genuine terror and clearly imagining a giant chicken just outside the back door, "No! There's *no* chicken outside," until one evening, my sister-in-law was visiting.

"Mommy?"

"Yes, Anna."

"No. There's *no* chicken outside!"

"No, honey, there's no chicken outside." I turned to my sister-in-law. "She's been saying that for months like she's afraid there's some huge chicken waiting outside the door."

"Deborah, you keep saying I'm going out to get the chicken."

"What?"

"On the grill. The BBQ is right outside and you keep saying you're going out to get the chicken."

"Oh! Anna, I'm so sorry." Sometimes it takes someone looking in from the outside.

Then, these adorable children become teenagers and a parent just needs to hang on until it passes. When he was 16 years old, during an argument, Jeff said matter-of-factly, "Dad, nothing you have just said is even remotely correct."

Dad said, "That was very well phrased."

Jeff replied, "What's *that* supposed to mean?"

Ugh. And the whole time you're just trying not to burst out laughing because we all know teenagers have no sense of humor when it comes to themselves. Laughing at a teenager is like juggling with dynamite.

Nancy and I got out of the car and started walking around Lisdoonvarna. (Really, once you learn how to say Lisdoonvarna, you can't stop saying Lisdoonvarna.) We studied a little local history. On a census chart dated 1901 every single one of the town's inhabitants were listed along with their relationships in the family (head of family, wife, son, etc), their religious affiliation (not surprisingly 100% Roman Catholic), their education level listed as one of these possibilities: Read-Write, Can Read, or Cannot Read; their marital status, their county of birth, and then, the last column where you could indicate one of four options: Deaf & Dumb, Dumb, Blind, Idiot or Lunatic. Yup. Not very PC in those days. Also listed was an occupation for every entry. In 1901, in Lisdoonvarna, the good folks' options were: Farmer, Farmer's Son, Policeman's Wife, Domestic Servant, General Labourer, Agriculture Labourer, Shop Keeper, Lodge Keeper, Boot Maker, Postman, Baker, Victuallyer, Coachbuilder, Barmaid, and that was pretty much the extent of it. Reading this list really gave us a feeling for what life was like in 1900 here.

We noticed the entry for Mary Glynn, 52 years old, wife of Patrick Glynn, listed with seven children — four girls and three boys. Under the occupation column Mary wrote "Mother of the Family." Of all the other mothers listed she was the *only* one who identified Mother of the Family as her occupation. Every other mother on the census left occupation blank. Interesting. Got a feeling we would have liked Mary Glynn. It was illuminating how much could be learned from just a few facts. Mary married Patrick, who worked for the railroad. They were Catholic. Their two older two boys, Patrick and John, both went to work in the fields as laborers. The older two daughters, Katie and Collin, both took jobs in their teens as domestic servants, and the younger three, Lizzie, Domis, and Mia, were in primary school in 1901.

Another family caught our eye — the Keighery family. The father, Thomas, was the postman. He and his wife, Bridget, who was 37 years old had children aged 16, 15, 14,12,11,8, and 3. Oh, my. I'm guessing Bridget Keighery didn't have an empty nest issue. By the time her youngest left home she simply collapsed. Life expectancy for women in that part of the world in 1900 was 50. Most women our age would be dead — empty nest problem solved.

The very light rain was clearing and we had hoped to see the Cliffs of Moher in the sunlight, so we hopped back into the car. Driving down the southwest coast a huge double rainbow formed directly in front of our car. We could see it from ground to ground. It was magical.

"So," Nancy asked, "what do you think? If we followed that rainbow and found the pot of gold what would you wish for?"

"Do I get to keep the pot of gold?"

"Unclear. Would we wish for our kids back?" Nancy asked.

"I don't want to go back in time. I don't actually know what I want."

"Maybe because moms don't spend much time thinking about what their personal wants are."

"I don't think I would go back. I am having fleeting moments where I feel ready to move on to new things, and then other moments when I feel really sad, physically, like something's sitting on my chest."

"Me, too."

"It's a weird situation. I don't want to go back, but I'm not sure I've given any attention to what going forward looks like."

"Well, we are heading for a cliff right now."

"Prophetic?"

"I hope not."

HEADING FOR THE CLIFF

The Cliffs of Moher jut up over 700 feet right out of the Atlantic Ocean. It is a sheer cut, an abrupt divide of land and sea. No need for beach, or foothills, or a slowly angled rise from the water – there is only down, down, down. On most days there is so much mist that the cliffs take on a sinister appearance, but when we arrived the sunlight was crisp and the ocean and sky were the same sapphire blue. The rolling waves were edged with frost white froth that looked like the lace trim on a pretty blue dress. The cliffs were dotted with a lime green moss and the confluence of the colors alone was worth the trip from home. Over a million people visit the cliffs in a year and only a lucky few get to see it in the sunlight – that day we were among the lucky and is was dramatic. We stood at the highest point in a small stone lookout tower, which was the only structure in sight. The Cliffs have been featured in everything from a Harry Potter movie to a Maroon 5 music video, but nothing can prepare you for standing there.

We considered how close to the edge we should go. We had been advised that sudden gusty winds can take a toll on those too close. In keeping with the Irish love of signs there were no shortage here. There was one of a stick figure plummeting off the cliff, one showing the cliff crumbling beneath a stick figure's feet, a large yellow exclamation point with the words "Extreme Danger," and one with a car plunging toward the water. There were signs whose intent was clear and signs that were completely baffling, like the one with a spinning wheel on it and an arrow. What was that supposed to mean? One sign, I suppose the grand-daddy of all, had 16 different icons on it. I swear if sign making goes out of style in Ireland half the population will be unemployed.

We cautiously stepped as close as we were comfortable. No one has a real count of the number of suicides or tourists who take a plunge here, but anyone who gets overly close to the edge has either no depth perception, or a death wish. Plenty of beauty can be seen and experienced from a few feet back. This was nature at its best, and it is our home planet in all her glory. Then, we turned and saw man-made at its best.

The Cliffs of Moher Visitors Center is a lesson in beauty and respect. A series of half-moon entranceways are carved directly into the natural hillside. No man-made object disrupts the incomparable exquisiteness of this scene. It blends seamlessly into the landscape and from every angle except directly in front it disappears completely. This is a visitor center worthy of sharing one of the most beautiful places on Earth. Every builder, architect, or designer, anywhere on our planet should be required to come and see this. We walked back to the car feeling lucky. Lisdoonvarna and the Cliffs of Moher in one day – new stories, new world.

We turned the car south and headed for Cork.

DON'T GO TO JAIL IN CORK

Cork is the third largest city in Ireland after Dublin and Belfast. It is traditionally noted that the city of Cork was founded by Saint Finbarr in the seventh century, but the area was inhabited long before that time and was actually a series of islands. Nancy and I were driving and frustrated as we looked for the historic 200-year-old Imperial Hotel on South Mall. It stood in the middle of a very busy city street, which was unfortunately one-way; it seemed one-way against us no matter which way we came. While we were close, only a block away, we simply could not seem to get there.

"I said left. Turn left. It's over there," Nancy said, frustrated, as we made our third circle around the center of Cork.

"It's one way again," I said. "Damn."

"No! Stop! That's a pedestrian area."

"Maybe I can get through that alley," I wondered.

"An alley, we can't even figure out the streets," Nancy reminded me. "Look out!"

"Okay," I admitted, "the alley wasn't my best idea."

"You can't go that way. Back up. It's one way. You have to circle."

"That's it. I'm done. Irish Park?"

"Irish Park," Nancy agreed.

I pulled the car to the side, double-parked, put on the flashers and we got out.

"Think they'll tow us?" Nancy asked.

"I don't get the feeling they're quite that organized in this city, but let's take our suitcases just in case. Now, see aren't you glad we only have one rolling bag?"

"Still, no." Nancy shook her head.

We found the Imperial Hotel a block away. Helen, at the reception desk, gave us directions to the car park. "From where you are make two lefts, go down and back, left again to the river and turn right, and then around the block to the entrance alley way, on the left-ish side, park, then, you'll have to walk along the upper bridge way to..."

"Um, Helen?" Even when Nancy's impatient she has this niceness to her tone.

"Yes." Helen was so cheerful.

"We've just spent half an hour trying to find our way around four streets."

"Oh, yes, it can be challenging. I'll show you." And with that she popped out from behind reception, strutted out to the street with us following, and hopped into the back seat of our car.

Would never happen in the U.S. There are too many rules. Surely there were liability rules, or rules about not leaving your post, or rules about not driving with strangers, or getting into a car with a hotel guest. The U.S. is an entire nation of orderly people who follow the rules and who stand in line. Now, I wouldn't try to *cut* in line – we've got a tight trigger on that one. I must say though I do not miss all the rules.

As Helen guided us through the streets toward the

car park she said, "I'm glad to get out for a moment. I'm nervous today."

"Why is that?" Nancy asked.

"My fiancé and I have a meeting with the priest to find out if we're compatible."

I was curious, "Oh? Is he a family friend?"

"No. Don't know him."

"Your fiancé knows him?" I asked

"No."

"Have you been dating long?" Nancy pressed.

"A couple of years," Helen replied.

"And you don't know if you're compatible?" It all sounded so odd to me.

"Oh, we are, we're in love. The meeting's mandatory. We already completed the Marriage Preparation Course."

"There's a prep course?" I asked.

"And we filled out the Pre-Nuptial Enquiry form, so the meeting is all that's left."

"There's a course *and* a form?" I said.

Nancy asked politely, "Is it a personality test, or like a therapy session?"

I added, "Or does one of you get thrown into the river to see if you float?"

"Ignore my sister, her sense of humor is an acquired taste."

Helen giggled. She was particularly amiable, red-cheeked, with a small grin, "Only a ten-minute meeting with the priest."

"And what if," I asked, "after this in depth ten-minute interview, he says you're not compatible?"

Her eyes clouded, "Oh, that can't happen, can it?"

Nancy jumped in, "Of course not." She gave me a warning look.

But I couldn't stop. "I would like to get a look at the

Marriage Prep Course syllabus. I could write the shit out of one of those."

"Helen, Deborah and I have both been married for over 20 years. Don't let her fool you. Marriage has been great for both of us."

"So, what's your advice then?"

I said, "Works best if *you're* blind and *he's* deaf."

Nancy rolled her eyes at me. "Oh, perfect."

"Oh, is that right?" Helen asked.

"Well, if the wife is blind she can't see that the husband is constantly messing everything up, and if the husband is deaf there's no limit to how long he'll listen to her."

"Again," Nancy said to Helen, "she's an acquired taste."

"What?" I protested, "I think that's great advice."

Nancy looked warmly at Helen, "Good advice is to always keep in mind marriage is a marathon: relationships take stamina ."

"My advice was better. No wait. Helen, I've got an important marriage story to tell you."

"Deborah, I think you've said enough," Nancy said.

"No, I'm serious."

"I'm listening," Helen said.

"When we were first married my husband had a really important meeting very early one morning. He popped out of bed and 5:00 a.m. and was getting ready. He was young and feeling a lot of anxiety about doing well. I was aware he was up and all, but it was 5:00 in the morning so I was buried under the covers. Suddenly, I heard him banging around and he said loudly, 'I *cannot* believe you're not helping me.' I could hear the frustration in his voice and so I bolted out of bed and went to him sleepy-eyed. 'What? What is it? What can I do?'

'I can't believe you're not helping me iron this shirt.'

"I was groggy, and of course I wanted to help, so I took the iron. 'Sure. I got this.'

"He ran to shave. Well, he assumed, I suppose because I was a woman, that I had some inherent ironing gene. And in my defense it was 5:00 in the a.m., as I may have mentioned, and I had never ever ironed a shirt in my life –I'm kind of a wash-n-wear girl."

"There's an understatement." Nancy grinned.

"I put the iron on the white shirt and hung around for a dazed moment and then...I slid the iron off to see a brown mark imprint the shape of the iron on the shirt. I was standing there staring at it trying to un-blurry my eyes and figure out what the hell happened when Larry ran back in. He looked at the shirt, gasped, said nothing, and ran back to the closet. Okay, but here's the good part. Helen, here's the part you want to remember. It's been over 20 years and he has *never* asked me to iron another thing."

"Oh," Helen nodded thoughtfully. "I see. I see."

"Now that's some damn good advice that you just won't find on a Prep Form."

Our room at the Imperial Hotel was lovely. The gold and white wallpaper made the room look cheerful and regal as well. The hotel had left a bottle of wine and two large chocolate cookies for us on the little table.

Nancy smiled, "Remember when we'd leave out milk and cookies for our kids after school? This is the adult version of that."

"Should we open the wine?"

"Later." She opened her suitcase.

"Have you noticed we're calling the kids less frequently?" I asked. "We're probably not annoying them as much."

"Yeah. And I also find when we do call I'm doing a lot

of the talking for a change." Nancy methodically hung up her shirts one-by-one, in a neat line.

"I noticed that, too." I said. "Until this trip, I think every conversation I've had with my kids has been a download or discussion about their experiences, their relationships, their complaints, or their successes. It has never been much of a two-way street and I never thought about it. I didn't care. I was interested."

"The mom-kid communication gets hard-wired that way because when they first went to kindergarten and they came home all I wanted was to hear every single minute of their day."

"Me, too."

"It grew from there. They came home from school and it was 'How was school today' and you got the stories of which teacher was mean, which kid was cheating, and which kid had a better sandwich at lunch."

"And material from their lives never slowed down because they were growing and having new experiences every day." I threw a couple of shirts on a chair and felt sufficiently unpacked.

"This is the first time that the story of my day is more remarkable than theirs," said Nancy, who looked sideways at my little bunch of clothing on the chair.

"They want to know where we are, what we're doing, they're involved because we're exciting, because we aren't exactly where they left us; eating the same food - in the same place - with all the same people - getting up at the same time - with the same plan as yesterday. My life was standing still and I didn't even recognize it. Nancy, it's no wonder we were relegated to always listening. We had nothing new to add after, "Mom, how are you?"

"I like my life, Deborah."

"I know. I know. But now I suppose I doubt whether my life, looking ahead, is enough for me as it is. I don't want to stand still anymore. I've been standing still for too long."

"You better appreciate what you have."

"I do, but I've got to tell you, I'm a long way from wanting to go back home to it."

"That sounds a little scary."

"But this is important. To know this. To understand that adding new experiences to life is what will keep us interesting and interested. It doesn't need to be as dramatic as leaving the country, but if what is new in our lives is no longer coming from the experience of raising our children, then we need to actively reach for something else; without new experiences we will have no stories to tell. Nothing to add to the conversations of our lives. We'll be listeners. The listeners of life. I don't want to be a listener."

"Clearly you don't want to be an un-packer either."

"You couldn't help it? Right? You had to say something."

"Yup."

Searching for something with the look and feel of history we headed for the Bells of Shandon – a bell tower at St. Anne's church in the old part of Cork. There you can ring the old bells and look out 360 degrees around Cork.

St. Anne's is perched on the top of a hill accessed by a cobbled uneven street. This was a sneakers required trek with the added fun of shin splints later. There has been a church on this spot since medieval times. This current structure was erected in 1722. The church had a tall square stone tower with a clock on each of the four sides. We walked up the entrance stairs and stepped into the tiny church antechamber. The walls were pocked and shredded in exactly the way I'd hoped.

History you can see and feel and smell – smell? Oh, no, that's the man at the desk. He was lunching on something fishy and pungent. I decided not to ask.

"Well, hello, young ladies."

Instantly, we liked the crooked gray-haired man. He wiped his mouth with a cloth handkerchief.

"Here to ring the bells, are you?" he asked.

"Yes."

"Need a donation to the church – six euro." We put the euros into the basket and I started for the stairs when he said, "Are you Irish, then?"

I said, "On our mother's side."

"Yeah? What's the last name?"

"Kelly," Nancy replied.

"You and everyone else." He let out a big guffaw. I understood this. I have a family full of people who find *themselves* funny. Nancy wasn't sure what he was laughing at. He continued. "Bet you girls don't know how to spell it."

We exchanged a quick look both knowing we were reacting to being called girls. It made us smile. Nancy really hates the ma'am thing.

"This is how you spell it." He took out a pencil and wrote "Ceallaigh" on the church flier.

"Oh." I took the paper from him. "We didn't know. Is that Kelly in Irish?"

"Certainly is. The famous Irish Fairy was named Kelly – Catherine Kelly. When she died at 29 years old in 1785 she was 34 inches tall."

"Tiny," Nancy said.

"That she was." He asked, "Do you know why they call the clock tower here the four-faced liar?"

"No." I folded the flier into my pants pocket. This was the kind of souvenir I liked - the unintended one.

"Because it has a clock on each of the four walls, but

they never tell the exact same time. Except when they hit the hour and then they're aligned again."

"Why is that?" Nancy asked

"Some folks say it's because of the wind, or the angle of the hands, or the thickness of the wood, but I know it's Saint Anne, her very self, reminding us that we are only human and do not control time."

I was beginning to wonder if I could fit this guy in my suitcase.

"Here." He handed us each a set of headphones (in case the sound was too much) and pointed to the wooden stairs. "Up you go. Watch your step. Watch your head. Watch your language – you're in church you know." He winked at us.

Climbing up we found the stairs were impossibly narrow and unevenly worn. Thoughtfully they had run a rope along the wall as a needed handhold. The walls of the tower at the base are seven feet thick and the climb to the top 120 feet.

Inside the bell room, there were taut ropes leading to the actual bells. There are eight bells comprising an octave and weighing over six tons. They rang for the first time on the 7th of December in 1752.

The bells are inscribed with the following:

1: *When us you ring we'll sweetly sing*

2: *God preserve the Church and King*

3: *Health and prosperity to all our benefactors*

4: *Peace and good neighbourhood*

5: *Prosperity to the city and trade thereof*

6: *Abel Rudhall, in 1750, cast us all at Gloucester in England*

7: *Since generosity has opened our mouths our tongues shall sing aloud its praise*

8: *I to the Church the living call and to the grave do summon all*

A visitor could pull the ropes and play the church bells. The curators had posted some sheet music so you could actually play something simple like Jingle Bells, or Three Blind Mice, if you were inclined. This is not a bustling tourist spot, but I'm sure they get a trickle all day long. And there was something very cool about handling these old ropes. Sometime later, though, I will not be surprised to hear that a quiet and unimposing Irish woman broke down the door to the church and smashed these bells in a wanton frenzy. There are residences all around this church – only yards away. These people are subjected to the cacophonous din of tourists playing one line of Waltzing Matilda ad infinitum. Can you imagine? It would drive me mad. I would rather live next to a dog kennel or the circus.

As mothers, we are experienced in the realm of auditory assaults. Jeff took a run at the piano, the saxophone, and the guitar. Olivia took up the drums, and then the next year she rehearsed at the top of her lungs for a solo (we cannot *believe* they gave her) in *Singing in the Rain*, a show we also could not *believe* they were still performing, and we had to sit through three times. Still, there was nothing that pinched your auditory nerves quite like the middle school choral recital. Teachers, why? I'm convinced it is some kind of revenge against all the parents that drive the teachers nuts. They set up these lengthy choral shows featuring a room full of no-talent kids at that awkward stage where they were gangly and self-conscious, where their faces were pimply, their hormones raging, and their teeth a construction zone so half of them were spitting as they sang. And some nefarious music teacher told them loud – sing loudly. And for an hour and a half you sit and smile at the atonal spitting display hoping not to get any on you.

Once I chaperoned when the middle school took the kids on a bus to a retirement home. The little room filled with elderly residents and the kids began their "concert." It was bad, and not a little bad, bad like shingles bad. A few jaws dropped open, well, maybe they were already open. I looked around and realized this was why they go to old folks homes, because most of the audience wasn't ambulatory. The people were trapped listening to these kids (my kid included) butcher every Christmas carol and Chanukah song ever written. How could they all be this tone-deaf? Thirty-five minutes into a 90-minute show some elderly lady had had enough. She was in a middle seat in the second row and she did not care. She stood up, grabbed her walker and started banging her way out. She hit the rows of chairs on either side of her, back and forth aggressively to clear a path, and she ploughed through with impressive determination. The teachers and two other mothers were aghast. Me? I understood, which didn't make me any new friends, but seriously? How could you blame her? She'd been told there was a concert in the meeting room.

Nancy and I ate that night at the bar in a place called Broadway that we could walk to from the hotel. It was fine casual food and suited us. The hotel room was pleasant and the beds comfortable. We thought about opening the wine that had been left but decided to keep it for another evening.

We slipped between the bed sheets, watched some cooking show, which I thought would surely put me to sleep. What could be more stupefying than watching water boil? Nancy drifted to sleep. I turned the TV off and lay awake for at least two eons.

I know sleep issues are common. Lots of people have them. My son, Jeff, is a sleepwalker, and we've established that Nancy screams. But it is so exasperating to want to sleep and be awake, too tired to do anything, not able to slip into sleep, lying there bored to the bone. This night the few lines of a song played over and over – and it was a song I don't particularly like. I rolled back and forth, went to the bathroom five or six times, turned on the light from my phone and tried to read under the covers. Sometimes it feels deeply lonely – like I'm the only person in the world who is awake. Sometimes I get mad and I kick the bed a few times. I know that's counterproductive so I try to talk to myself down, suggesting various relaxation methods: the rushing water technique, the contract and relax muscles technique, the thinking of clouds, or numbers, the repeating a calming word or phrase - nothing works. It is either a tribute to my naïveté or to my desperation that I keep trying these; but then, what the hell else am I going to do in the middle of the night – I got time.

The following morning we took the bus tour, which was full of history and information and no insulting jokes from 1950 about the driver's wife. This was the best bus tour we had in Ireland. We stopped at the Gaol (jail/prison) and decided to go inside. Nancy and I do genuinely like creepy places. Architecturally it was a spectacular building, a U-shaped, all stone impenetrable looking structure. Cork Gaol opened in 1824 and closed in 1923 – one hundred years of humans incarcerated in dire conditions for crimes committed or imagined. For a time it was used solely for women. What were their crimes? How were they treated? What was life like here? Will we feel it once inside? We were energized as we entered the building speculating about the history and the intrinsic drama of this place. When I indicated that Nancy and I genuinely liked creepy places, perhaps I should have said we liked genuine creepy places – this place had been so fabricated to appeal to a family of tourists that it had lost its claim to genuineness and substance. This prison was part wax museum, part multimedia show, part gift shop, and disinfected from any historical context whatsoever. It felt like a good place to bring the kiddies and isn't that really what you're looking for in a prison – an appropriately sized area for a bounce tent? They actually host a Family Fun Day, yes, with bounce tent. On Thursday nights, you can take the "ghost" tour – complete with a guarantee of ghosts and bumps in the dark. There was some talk about a daring great escape, which went like this: a few guys climbed over the wall one night. Yeah, that's the entire story – a few guys climbed over the wall one night. We were not impressed. The value of historical places lies in their authenticity. Everything here was staged.

"Shall we blow out of here?" Nancy said indignantly.

"Are you sure you don't want to stop by the gift shop and pick up a little trinket of absolutely no value?"

"They probably have a little plastic gallows that plays "Danny Boy"."

"There's a souvenir for the kiddies."

We spent our last evening in Cork in a sweet and rambling mood, wandering with no agenda, no list, no plan, walking for the sake of walking. We split a bottle of wine at dinner and ambled around the streets near the hotel recounting childhood memories and wishing that our sister Eileen could have come with us. If we'd known in advance how meaningful this journey was going to be then we would have insisted she leave her husband, her huge corporate job, and her two sophisticated daughters, Elena and Julia, and join us for at least a little while.

The next day we planned to drive through Cobh (pronounced Cove) where our grandmother's mom boarded a ship bound for New York, and where the Titanic made its last stop. Then, on to Nancy's one non-negotiable stop: Ballyknocken Cookery School. She was psyched.

Turning the corner toward the hotel we passed by a little shop. In front there was a blackboard sign with a message written in chalk. This was by far our favorite sign in a country with an obsession for signs. It said simply, and with every expectation that the passerby would understand, "Wanted Flies Dead or Alive."

DROWNING OR STARVING IN COBH

Cobh is a seaport town on the southeast coastal tip of Ireland. Over a million Irish men and women departed for North America from exactly where we were standing now. It used to be named Queenstown, and it was here on a cold night in 1890 that our great-grandmother, Ellen, running away from an arranged marriage with some old fart of a guy, hopped a boat for The Big Apple and a new life. She was 21 years old, so about the same age our children. Ellen had never been anywhere, never done anything until she stepped on that boat. Was she scared to go, or scared to stay? How desperate must you feel to take that kind of step? Or how naive? What would she think of her two great grand-daughters standing here staring out at the freezing grey water that she had trusted with her life?

Nancy said, "She stood here and turned away from everyone she had ever known."

"I cannot imagine."

"Knowing she was never coming back. Wondering if she'd even survive the voyage and still willing to step onto that boat."

We couldn't take our eyes off the water; it was not invitingly blue like the Pacific we knew, it was a metallic viscous angry liquid.

I remembered, "Mom told me she had a sister she left behind in Sligo."

"A sister?"

"At least one, but maybe more."

"She must have been so miserable," Nancy said, "and lonely to have no emotional ties to her mom, her dad, or her siblings; so detached she was content to just sail away. How does a family let that happen?"

"And then produce us a family like ours — all tangled up inside each other's lives?"

"Maybe that's what Ellen was hoping for when she stepped onto that ship."

"And here you and I stand together right now, so maybe she achieved it."

"I do like to think about her that way."

We sat down on a park bench facing the Celtic Sea. We were quiet for a few minutes, experiencing our imaginations in real time with no distractions. The wind was cool enough to make our eyes glassy and the sea rolled around alive and restless. The quiet was inside. We felt nostalgia for someone we never knew. I was glad we had planned the trip in this order, so by the time we arrived at Cobh the momentum of our lives had slowed enough for us to be content to tarry, lost in thought, imagining a young woman of another time and feeling a genuine connection to her. We did feel it. Ellen stood right here, looked at the same thing we're seeing right now, and then, by stepping off this island began a series of events that led directly to us right here.

Nancy asked me, "Do you remember her at all?"

"I was six years old when she died; she was in her

nineties. I recall something of her voice. The accent, I think. I remember vaguely a birthday party of some kind for her. I think she was in a wheelchair. That's all." I shrugged.

Nancy turned to face me. "I didn't know I was going to feel something here, but I do. It's strange. Strange and deep."

"Yes. Yes, it is."

Cobh is one of the most beautiful little cities we've ever seen. It is spotless. In the Irish tradition, the buildings alternate in lively colors: yellow, red, blue, green, beige. Across the street and along the seafront a promenade winds alongside an ornate gazebo, which was crafted with elaborate detail, and at that moment had several small boys running around it.

Cobh has one of the world's largest natural deep-water harbors, and so this is where the cruise ships dock. On April 11, 1912 it was the final port for the Titanic. Cobh has a museum dedicated to the Titanic tragedy, which still holds a fascination for so many. Inside were wall-sized striking black and white photographs. Here, on that April day, an additional 123 ill-fated travelers boarded and joined the doomed. Evidently, there was one — just one guy who got off here — one very lucky Irish guy.

In the Titanic's original port of Southampton, England, a 23-year-old Irishman, John Coffey, was hired on as a stoker. It was a strenuous and filthy job shoveling coal into the burners and he didn't much care for it. So, when the Titanic docked at Cobh and they began tendering items back and forth to shore John deserted. He hid underneath the mail sacks going ashore, and made his way back to his family home nearby. It is hard to know at what point the crew noticed they were short one hand – but then they had other looming issues.

Nancy said, "According to this, John Coffey hid under the mail sacks."

"Yeah?"

"Those must have been the last letters ever written by these people. And since the Titanic didn't sink until four days later all those letters must have been on their way already. I wonder if people got letters a week later from their drowned relatives?"

"Pretty dark, Nancy."

"Would be very dark."

We moved onto the Irish heritage section of the museum. It focused on Ireland Emigration & Famine. Here we were treated to photos and information on the scope and devastation of the potato famine.

I actually like history. I like it a lot. I know Nancy does, too. But we had just spent an hour re-living the terror of the Titanic, and now we'd moved into millions of people starving to death. This was not an uplifting kind of place. We decided to take a short break and then maybe give it another try.

The Cobh Heritage Museum is located in the Railway Station and it is a lovely old brick building with a glass roof and a number of small bistro tables. We took a little table at the café, got a bottle of water, and split the cookie we'd saved from the Imperial Hotel.

"No one writes letters anymore," Nancy said.

"I like the feel of a letter. It was always kind of thrilling to go to the mailbox and find a surprise. Email killed that. I know it's more efficient and I keep in touch with more people, but something tactile is lost."

"Last time I remember getting a letter was when the kids went to camp. No electronics were allowed and they had prescribed letter writing times. I still have all those letters."

"So do I, in a plastic bin on the shelf of my closet."

Nancy said, "Camp didn't work out for my kids."

"Mine either. And Larry was disappointed because he loved camp as a boy and wanted them to have the same experience, so we sent them to where he went in Minnesota. They were wretched the entire time. The letters were so melodramatic, you would have thought we sent them to a work camp."

"The summer that I sent Nicole to camp I got a letter which was one line: 'Mom, did you *know* there are flying bugs here?'"

"Yeah, it's hard for Southern California kids to go away in the summer, the humidity and the bugs are impossible for them. You and I were used to it growing up in New Jersey. One time I got a one line letter from Jeff, he was about eight, and when I pulled it out of the envelope it looked like it had been crunched into a ball and then smoothed out again. It said: 'Mom, got in a fight with Taylor who scrumbled up my paper, and then I got it back. Love Jeff.'"

Nancy remembered, "The one time Matt went to camp he called me the first afternoon. I was so surprised since cellphones were not allowed. He told me he talked the cook into letting him call and he begged me to come back and get him. Then, I don't know how, but the next three days he got the cook's phone every afternoon, called, and begged me to come get him. Finally, on day four, the phone rang and he said very theatrically: 'This is it, Mom. The cook said no more. I will never be talking to you again.' That's when the letters started, and they weren't any happier. We never sent either one of the kids to camp again, but I kept the letters."

"I haven't looked at those letters in ten years. I think I'll pull them out when I get home."

"Let's do it together. We can call a couple of girlfriends, open several bottles of wine, and read our kids camp letters out loud," I said.

"Family theater."

"So fun, right?"

"Yeah. Love it." We finished the cookie. "Hey, do you know what day it is? Is it a Wednesday?"

"No clue."

"Huh, interesting."

"C'mon let's go look at some more death and destruction in the Cobh Museum – want to continue with drowning or move onto starvation?"

"Let's take a shot at starvation."

We walked together slowly around the exhibits. We read the plaques and the information guide. The potato blight began in 1845 with a crop failure and was followed for a couple of years with more failures. It led to the starvation of over a million people and the emigration of a million more. Children, who were barely skeletons, dropped over dead in the fields and towns. People ate grass. The more we read the more we wanted out of this museum. It was too horrific, too graphic. These were images I simply didn't want in my mind. I didn't feel like we needed to relive this in such detail.

"Nancy, are you ready to go?"

"Definitely. I can't take any more of this history lesson."

"God damn, Brits, you know," yelled out the man beside us.

We turned. Next to us was a lanky, toothless, freckled man, on crutches and looking exceedingly worn for being around 40 years old. He was showing his 13-year-old son, Collum, the museum. Collum had obviously never seen a hungry day in his life.

He continued speaking directly to us. "You gotta understand what happened here. You gotta understand the limey's in the nest."

We're not different from most people who want to leave a good impression when they travel. So, we nodded and smiled, gave a little uh huh, and hoped that would suffice. Not a chance. This was an Irishman with a story to tell. We have Irish uncles and knew any hope of a quick retreat was futile. The Irish are, always have been, always will be, storytellers.

Nancy said, "It says here the potatoes were diseased and that's why the crop failed."

"That's right. That's right there, but that ain't no way why the Irish starved. Oh, they're related mind you, but it was the Brits at the bottom of it."

"Of course, we realize there is a lot of unresolved conflict between the Irish and the English," I tried, "but I don't think the British unleashed a disease in 1845 to kill the potatoes."

"Are you sure you want to get into this?" Nancy whispered.

"Well, he's teaching his son this history, so I'm wondering what he's learning." I turned to the man, "What do you mean?"

"Yeah. Well, I'll tell you. Collum, listen up while I inform these foreigners on what really happened."

Collum opened up his rolling suitcase, which from a quick glance looked like it was full of Cheetos, and he pulled out a candy bar that was the size of a legal pad and went at it. The irony was lost on his dad.

"A conspiracy. They took a tax, you see. It was their way of killing us and keeping their hands clean, you see? No one had any money to pay the taxes these Brits were chargin' us, and so they took it in fish, or lamb, or whatever else you had, until you had nothin' left 'cept potatoes." He continued red-faced with rising anger. "Then the potato crop failed and folks starved 'cause they had nothing 'cause they gave it all to the god damn Brits! They knew. They knew exactly what they were doin'."

The bitterness in his tone was so fresh it sounded like it happened last year and not 150 years ago.

"I see," said Nancy with polite finality.

"Ah, wait a minute here," I began, "so..."

Nancy interrupted, "Deborah?"

"I was just thinking..."

As she turned away she said to the man. "Thank you. I hope you like the tour."

"Like it!" He was practically yelling, "People starved!"

Nancy called this one right and we headed for the door as she asked me, "Did you really want to get into a history argument with that guy and his adolescent Hoover?"

"Really, I have always wondered how people living this close to the ocean, with all the free food in the ocean, could starve by the millions? I've always kind of thought – get a fishing pole. I was interested in this tax thing."

"Okay, well, I'd suggest a reputable scholarly article instead of that really angry guy."

"Yeah. Sounds reasonable."

It was hard to leave Cobh in spite of the morbid exhibits. It was hard to head away from such a beautiful town. It was hard – actually – since we found ourselves at the top of a very skinny, very steep, one-way street to realize we were going the wrong way. The problem became clear when at the crest of the hill a car was coming at us.

"Oh, shit." Nancy closed her eyes.

"We may have done something wrong here. Did you see a sign? Nancy, open your eyes."

"It's so much more relaxing if I don't."

Now I was stopped and the other car was stopped facing each other. There was no room to turn around and no room to pull over. Buildings lined the street on both sides. We were just at that point at the top of a hill where we couldn't see over the lip. The man at the wheel opposite us pointed indicating I should back up. And so I shifted to reverse, craned my neck, and began to back all the way down this hill the length of a football field. It was harrowing and I can't deny I might have nudged a trash can or two along the way. It wouldn't have been so stressful if so many people hadn't stopped to watch. We backed out onto the main street along the water, embarrassed since we'd garnered so much attention. At least 20 locals had stopped to watch us back down this hill, which only made it harder. I could feel them wishing for a dramatic conclusion and I was committed to not providing it. I inched back.

"Seriously," I was annoyed, "don't these people have anything to do?"

"They are doing something. They're being entertained by your driving."

"Hey, Nance, if you want to take the wheel…"

"Not when you're entertaining so many people. Really, Deborah, it's a gift."

"Well, I'd like to reiterate that *you* are the navigator. I'm just trying to stay on the right side of the road, so technically direction is your area. So the fact that we're going backwards right now is on you."

"It's worth it to see you crank your head around that far for this long. You should be thanking me for getting you this great neck stretch. So good for the body."

"Just dig out the Advil."

We arrived at the flat area on the bottom of the main road.

"Make a U-turn," Nancy said.

"Is that legal?"

"It's that, or park in the middle of this street."

"Right."

I made a three or eight-point U-turn. Two teenaged boys broke out in applause and we drove quickly away. We made our way out of Cobh and headed for Ballyknocken Cookery School in Wicklow. We decided to take the longer of the two routes up the eastern coast because it would take us through Waterford. Nancy had seen a photograph of a bridge she was interested in seeing. We were back on the road.

DAMSELS IN DISTRESS

Get a dog. When we first started considering how we would feel when our last child took the speed ramp out of our daily lives a friend suggested I get a dog. She was the same friend who suggested I get a dog when my last dog died, when Larry traveled for work, when my closest friend moved out of town, and when I was complaining about the moles in my backyard. It was her Go To answer. I thought about it. I did consider it. I love dogs. In most ways, I prefer dogs to people. I've had three family dogs and fostered numerous for the animal shelter nearby. Getting a puppy would seem a natural answer to the impending vacancy in my home. Nancy still had her dog, but Hobie was old now and his requirements were minimal. Basically, he sleeps blissful on the kitchen tile ruminating on what a fabulous life he's had.

"Did you think about getting a puppy?" I asked Nancy.

"Hobie wouldn't be happy with a little puppy running all over the place. Too much commotion for him at his age."

"I thought about it, but I didn't feel up for training anyone else on the ins-and-outs of proper peeing protocols."

In the past six months, it seemed Nancy and I were overly focused on what we were losing and not at all on what might be gained.

"We've been caretakers for a really long time."

"Twenty years." Nancy pulled out the map. "Aren't we due for a gold watch or something?"

"I kind of like getting up in the morning and not having to arrange, or plan, or worry, about anything or anyone else. And I don't feel guilty anymore about it. I'm just loving not knowing what I'll see or do tomorrow."

Nancy said, "Next stop Waterford."

"You know what I love about this country? Look."

Coming into view about 50 yards from the road in a field surrounded by nothing else was a lone square tower. It stood about four or five stories high, constructed completely of different sized stones fitted together and settled in place for probably 700 years since this was clearly an actual medieval structure. There were six long skinny slots going up along the face, which I supposed served for light, as lookouts, and as a secure place to launch arrows at an advancing enemy. Europeans, who live with these remnants of times past, cannot appreciate the wonder it produces in we travelers from the "new" world where history is counted on a much smaller yardstick. Nancy and I had seen a number of stone structures as we'd crossed Ireland, but this one was invitingly close. We could walk to this one. I pulled the car over.

"C'mon. Let's take a closer look."

"And get some pictures."

We traipsed through the muddy ground that sucked at our sneakers. This was some kind of marsh. Maybe it was a river at one time. While the structure was mostly intact, moss and other greenery grew out from between the many stone joints. It was derelict and beautiful, masterfully built, and filled with voices and stories of another age. Here was the taste of medieval history I'd hoped for from the Abbeyglen Not-A-Castle Castle. My heart was pounding and I couldn't contain my enthusiasm. This was even better than a castle made for tourists – this was real, a lost structure, forgotten, left behind, and not dressed up for company. I touched the stones.

"There doesn't seem to be a castle or monastery around here that this was part of, so this must have been an outpost. Like some kind of keep, maybe?"

"A keep?"

"A keep was a defensible tower where people could hide from an advancing enemy and store food and weapons. Those long thin slots were not only to let in light, but to serve as a lookout, and just wide enough for a bow and arrow."

We took two pictures in front and then walked around to the side where we found an entrance, an iron spiked gate, with rods about six inches apart, and beyond it blackness. Nancy took another picture of the gate.

"Can you feel this?" I asked.

"Yes, so interesting."

Nancy took a few steps back to snap more pictures. I leaned against the gate – it gave. I looked. It was positioned to look closed but the hinge was damaged. One shove and I could be in there.

"Ah, Nance?"

"No."

"We can though."

"No."

"We have to."

"Do you see that sign? The big one right there? It says: 'WARNING – THIS IS PRIVATE PROPERTY. Unauthorized access by trespass is not permitted. No liability for trespassers is accepted by the owner and anyone who trespasses does so of their own risk.'"

"It's just a sign. Another Irish sign. There's no one around."

"What do you think they mean by that? You know, risk. If you were to take a wild guess what do you think they're trying to tell us?"

"Did we come here to follow the rules?" I asked.

"If they make sense."

"Aren't we tired of taking the safe route?"

"A little."

"We've been following the rules for years."

Nancy looked around. There was no one in sight. She said, "Let's just take a quick look and then on our way."

We pulled the gate away from the lower hinges where it was weak and slid past the two-foot thick walls and into the dark.

I took hold of the iron spokes. "Help me push back the gate in case someone drives by so they don't notice it open." And we did.

It took a moment for our eyes to adjust. It was an empty square room. About ten feet up, a few streams of narrow light came in through the skinny openings in the stone wall, and a chunk of the roof had fallen in throwing light into one corner and making the rest of the room look even darker in comparison. There was half of a floor high above us, but no ladder to get there.

"Must have been some kind of staircase here at some point."

"Maybe a wooden ladder," Nancy suggested. "See these wooden sticks on the ground."

"Yes. Let's just sit down on the floor for a couple of minutes and visualize what it was like to be alive then."

"You want to sit on the dirt?" Her eyes were wide and

most certainly disgusted.

"You got a date later and need those pants to be clean?"

"One of us insisted on a carry-on suitcase and my few clean clothes are precious to me."

"Uh, huh."

"Deborah, it is dark, damp, moldy, there are probably rats and bugs and at least 500 years of god knows what else on that floor including ancient entrails."

"Humor me."

"Can I humor you from a standing position?"

"Sure." I sat down on the dirt floor near one of the medieval walls. I closed my eyes to imagine.

Nancy appreciated that this mattered to me. She knew Abbeyglen had been a disappointment. This was that moment when your mother says, "Deb, get up off the ground"; when your husband says, "Honey, are you nuts?"; when your kids say "Ooh, that's gross," but when your sister takes one second, and then sits right down beside you, and waits for you, silently. And my sister let me sit there quietly for a good ten minutes without a word.

Yes, I know it's weird, but I touched the floor and closed my eyes and tried to put myself back there. There was a very light wind blowing through the upper level and the smell of dirt and moss and yesterday was thick. I felt there. I was so happy. I heard the sounds of horses hooves approaching as people came and went. I felt connected. People travel into the wilderness and they talk about the need to feel connected to the earth and to nature. I have a need to feel connected to an earlier humanity. It thrills me and calms me at the same time. And it was even better since this was not a fake or staged place. We were somewhere we were not allowed, a place abandoned, and frozen in time.

I whispered, "Fabulous. What was it like to live then? To *be* them."

"Dirty," Nancy said.

"Yeah."

"Cold."

"For sure."

"People bathed once a year and crapped out the window."

"Charming," I said.

"Do you know why they had lap dogs?" Nancy asked.

"Why?"

"The ladies used to hold dogs on their laps to lure the fleas off themselves. That's how they got their name."

"Nance, you're kind of destroying the mood."

"Just a little reality check."

"Well, I loved this moment."

"I'm glad. Let's get going. I want to find Wicklow before dark and we still need to get through Waterford."

So, I said goodbye to the history, which felt so real right here. And we left. Well, we went to leave.

"Push."

"No," Nancy said, "pull because we pushed to get in."

"Oh, yeah, that's right." So I pulled. No movement.

Nancy looked at me. Her eyebrows went up.

I said, "We just need to pull together."

"Okay."

Both of us gripped the old iron spoke door and pulled. No movement. We bent down to look carefully at where the hinge had given on the way in, and saw that when we had pushed the gate back it became jammed on the wrong side of a little rock lip.

"Holy shit." Nancy rarely swore.

"Nancy, it only needs a little more pull that's all. Together. One, Two, Three."

And we yanked – nothing. We stepped back and our

situation sank in.

Nancy reminded me with a warning seriousness. "We are too far from the road for anyone to hear us."

"This is no big deal. Really." I looked at her face. "Okay, maybe it's a little deal."

"If we're trapped in here, Deborah, are we trapped in here?"

"No, of course, not. I mean it's crumbling so it's open at the top. We could always climb up and over and drop down."

"Climb up these rocks with no rope and drop down 40 feet?"

"Well, I'm not saying it'd be easy. No reason to panic," I said. "I'm sure there's a solution."

"Oh?"

"Sure. Last resort, we can call the police if we have to."

"My cellphone is in my purse – my purse is in the car."

"Oh," I realized. "Mine, too."

With a different kind of silence, we considered our options. Now, the room looked harsh and unforgiving.

"You know what this reminded me of?" I said.

"Why we should heed warning signs?"

"No. A few years ago this girl from the U.S. disappeared in Ireland. Teams searched, dogs, helicopters, Coast Guard. Her dad flew in from Georgia. Four days into the search someone spotted her wandering around inside a locked deserted stone building completely disoriented. She had no idea how she got there, how the door got locked, and couldn't remember anything of the last four days."

"Nice story. And great time to tell it. Exactly what I wanted to hear."

"It is interesting, you know, in an historical sense,"

I said, "because right now, we can kind of feel what it must have been like to be shut up away in one of these things."

"Are you serious?"

"They used to shut women away all the time in those days: if a man decided he didn't want to be married anymore; or if a woman couldn't have children; or if a younger more attractive girl came along. At this moment, we can better imagine what that might have felt like to have a door close you in like that. To feel like you couldn't get out."

"I am not slapping you right now because you're my sister. But I want you to know I'm holding back."

"I appreciate that. Still, we're living history."

"Holding back."

A few quiet moments passed. We scanned the enclosure and ran scenarios in our heads, looking for a route out of this dark hole.

"Eventually someone will see the car," I said.

"And so?"

"Don't you think someone will stop and wonder why it's parked there?"

"And by eventually do you mean in a week or two?"

"Yeah. Not optimal. Want to try and give me a foot hold up to that next level?"

"What for?"

"See what's up there?"

"Let's just stay on the ground where we know it's solid."

"Okay."

Nancy walked slowly around the interior and kicked over a few rocks and then pointed to the floor.

"Hand me that wood piece behind your foot."

I picked up a piece of wood about two feet long and gave it to her. She bent down and studied the bottom of the iron gate hinge just by the lip. She wedged the end of wood in there and pushed down forcefully.

"Good thinking," I said.

We took hold of the lever together.

Nancy said, "Everything we've got. One, two, three..."

We pressed hard on the lever jammed under the hinge where it had given before. It pulled apart. We both grabbed the loose rod and yanked it toward us. It created an opening wide enough for us to crawl through.

Gratefully on the outside again, we practically ran to the car. We hopped in. Nancy locked the doors, which made no sense, but still made us both feel better.

Nancy said, "We never leave the car without our phones in our pocket again."

"Never. I wasn't scared though."

"Me, either."

We grinned at each other, both of us lying.

The balance had shifted. We both felt this. The content of our thoughts and conversations were less about our past, our kids, and our lives as mothers, and more focused on where we were at the moment. And, yes, it had been an imposed change. We did toss ourselves out of the country. But when you're fighting for that t-shirt at Literary Pub Crawl, or wandering through jail in Cork, or stuck in a medieval tower, or maybe backing down a one-way street, your conversation naturally changes. It was forced, and although we didn't know it when we made our plans, it was incredibly effective. Everything was new, present, and demanded our attention because we were doing – we were not waiting – we were not visitors in someone else's life. We could miss our kids. We did. And yes the dynamics of our family living all under the same roof was forever changed, but there was a qualitative difference between missing and being left behind in life. We found that control was in our hands.

Nancy took lots of photographs, which she enjoyed so much that she decided she would certainly enroll in some workshops when she got home. She remembered seeing an ad for one in Arizona, which she had thrown out. It was a three-day affair, close enough for her to drive, and a very reasonable rate. She wasn't wondering if she should, if she could, or if it were practical. Why had turned into why not. And sometimes why-the-hell-not.

Physically flinging ourselves across the ocean awakened us to how small our world had become. We saw the boundaries in our lives. There was the occasional trip, but 90% of our days and nights happen within 15 miles of our home base. I read an article once that said the general world population never ventures farther than ten miles from their homes in their entire lives. It stuck with me because I remembered feeling sorry for them. But this is all of our truths, isn't it? Think about how often you traverse your every day perimeter and step outside your pattern. For us, traveling beyond our pattern allowed a clear view back at how confined we had been. How small our world was. We began this journey because we thought we had lost what there was to do, when now it was clear that we had so very much to do we had better get going. We were no longer running away but running to. Time was not laying out in front of us in a boring no-kid stretch, time was short; short to see new things, go new places, become new ourselves.

Nancy had seen photos of the River Suir Bridge in Waterford. It was a newly constructed cable-stayed bridge completed and opened about a year before our trip. Consequently, she had an idea of how it would look. I didn't. I remembered thinking, *a bridge?* Not that excited. Can't recall ever doing anything but shrugging at a bridge.

"What? Look. What is that?" I was awed.

As we approached, it looked like waving thin lithe arms, undulating gracefully. This was the second time in a week that something man-made in Ireland left us staggered by its artistry. The first time was the visitors center at the Cliffs of Moher, and now this. This was magnificent. It made the Golden Gate in San Francisco look like an ugly cousin. This bridge is 1,525 feet long, 98 feet wide, and 367 feet high, but those statistics do not tell the story. It is unimaginably thin. Elegant slender white arms fan out from the peak down with a stylish curving appearance that gives the impression of movement, and driving toward it on route N25 it appeared as though we were entering a tall skinny letter A. It was challenging to pull the car off the Waterford Bypass so Nancy could snap some photos, so I did the best I could, and then parked Irish. (Off to the side, flashers on) It was absolutely worth the detour. Neither of us had ever been fans of contemporary public architecture, which usually yields rectangular structures of unadorned concrete, metal, and glass – functional but not aesthetically pleasing in any way. It would be a benefit to future generations if the majority of modern day architects (and committees that hire them) were shot at dawn for lack of imagination. We appreciate murals, colorful glasswork, sculpture, mosaics, domes, maybe some clinker bricks – it doesn't have to mimic an old-fashioned style but it doesn't need to be devoid of artistic content either. There are young artists all over the world who would jump at the opportunity to create something, to paint a mural on the side of a building, to devote some time to a large public project – and starving artists are rarely expensive. Ireland had married the contemporary and the functional with absolutely stunning results. So, it was not that today's public buildings *must* be built with the directive of cheap and monotonous. The River Suir Bridge was finished ten months ahead of schedule, even though while building they happened upon an ancient Viking settlement, Woodstown, and had to reroute the approach to protect it. This is proof that it is not a lack of money that makes our city buildings tedious and ugly – it's a lack of vision or the will to follow it.

A CROCK OF COOKERY

Back on the road, we figured we would easily reach the Ballyknocken House & Cookery School before nightfall. Nancy cares about local fresh products. She knows what's in season, which spices go with what, and thoroughly enjoys the creative aspect of putting something colorful and tasty on her stylish table. She hadn't heard of this particular cooking school, but her research indicated that the chef had a popular TV cooking show in Ireland, and had written several successful books. It had become cool to go to these cooking schools in the last several years. We were both excited about the workshop tomorrow. We had done a lot of driving and observing so we were eager for something hands-on.

There has been an explosion of famous chefs and food-oriented television shows. The generation before us there was Julia Child and that was it. I don't know exactly how chefs became such celebrities. I'm not even clear at which moment they went from cooks to chefs, but it happened, and now they're everywhere. Food is everywhere. On the Travel Channel, on PBS, it even has its own Network – creatively called The Food Network. In the past decade or so we've had all kinds of amusing chefs burst onto the scene. The I-can-do-that-in-30-minutes Rachel Ray, the Barefoot Contessa (frankly, I don't know why she's barefoot, but if she's in the kitchen I suggest she put on her clogs), then there's Giada De Laurentiis who's adorable, but all that long loose hair while cooking, I'm thinking some guests are getting a little extra fiber with their meal. And what can be said about Paula Deen who got type-2 diabetes from eating her own high-fat, high-sugar, deep fried, butter globbed recipes, and then continued to promote those recipes anyway. Then, there are the guys. Adam Richman on *Man v. Food*, where he shows America just how much he can shove in his mouth, Bobby Flay who keeps his knives longer than his wives, and *Iron Chef America* with Alton Brown (who may be proof of extra-terrestrial life here). I find these shows really entertaining, and evidently so do others since they continue to proliferate.

Looking for Ballyknocken was the only time we got lost in Ireland. It was challenging to find this place. We had been given directions by the locals a few times, and even though we were certain this was an English speaking country, we couldn't piece together their responses. We called the Ballyknocken twice along the way and their directions kept mentioning a church we couldn't seem to find. We did eventually U-turn onto the correct road – mostly by process of elimination.

The Ballyknocken House & Cookery School was a couple of structures. The main house was a two-story, white, box-style home, with a glassed-in front porch area. Ivy crawled up some of the outside walls. Inside and through the porch to the little foyer we met a young lady who would take us to our room. The porch and foyer were cluttered, in a charming way, lived-in way. We peeked into the dining room, which was quaintly decorated although fairly cramped. I was uncertain how many people they usually served for meals, but there were about six small tables set up. I liked it. It felt homey. We knew the main house had a few guest rooms, but we were told we'd been upgraded to the apartment. That sounded good. Across the driveway, past the Kitchen Herb Garden, and into another structure we were shown to our room – or rather rooms. Two bedrooms! It would be our first night sleeping in separate rooms since we started. Each bedroom had its own bath – heaven. Down the hall was a kitchen with a table and chairs and a nice little sofa area. I was glad to know that if I had sleeping issues that night I could turn on the light and not worry about waking Nancy. Nancy was glad to know that any errant screams in the night would not be heard by anyone other than me. We left our stuff and we were out the door again moments later. We were really hungry. The other hotel guests were eating in the Ballyknocken dining room that evening, and we did glance longingly through the window as we loaded back into the car. Two nights at the Ballyknocken along with the four-hour cooking workshop had been our most expensive single event. We decided against adding on an extra dinner on arrival night when we learned that it was a fixed menu and about 70 dollars a person – ah, no. We were happy to buzz into town (wherever that was) that first night, and eat at the Ballyknocken the next day.

Town. Where was that? We didn't actually pass a town. We set off down the country road. It was eerily dark with no streetlights, which was a problem. The clues I had been using to stay properly on the "wrong" side of the road were impossible to see. My confidence level was low, but I was keeping it to myself. I didn't want to scare Nancy, although it was not lost on me that she was clenching her teeth and shaking her foot.

We had a fairly workable system going so we silently stuck with it. I wouldn't tell her when I was having trouble driving, and she wouldn't keep jumping out of her seat. Deal.

We had passed a Chinese place not far from the street that led up toward Ballyknocken. We had an apartment with plates and glasses. Instead of driving around, we decided to pick up some Chinese take-out, go back to our rooms, open the bottle of wine we brought with us from the Imperial Hotel in Cork and enjoy some lovely sisterly privacy in a nice homey environment. We pulled into the Chinese hole-in-the-wall and loaded up with take-out.

We snuck back into this gourmet cooking school hiding our Chinese take-out bag under our coat. We sprinted past the dining room windows and back into the apartment.

So, this is the question: How many determined women does it take to get into a bottle of Chardonnay if you have no corkscrew?

"Okay," Nancy said. "Let's think this through."

"Right."

The bottle stood in the middle of the kitchen table. We wanted it. So, so, badly.

Nancy continued. "There has got to be a way to open this bottle."

"Has to be."

We rummaged through the drawers in the kitchen for the fifth time. Still, no corkscrew.

Nancy picked up a knife. "We can try and push it into the bottle."

"Okay. I'll hold it you press."

"Mmmmmmmm." She pushed, not even close to budging. "Maybe if I stick the knife in and use that tea kettle over there like a hammer?"

"I'm game. I want that wine."

"Me, too."

Nancy stuck the knife in the cork. I held the bottle she took the iron tea kettle and smacked the top of the knife.

"The knife went farther in. It's stuck, but I don't think this cork is moving."

"Let me try." I yanked and yanked. Nothing. "I guess we could go to the main house and ask for a corkscrew."

"We told them we had dinner plans and that's why we weren't eating here."

"Yes, but..."

"Excuse me, but we have this free wine from another hotel and our Chinese take-out food here in your fancy foodie place so can we borrow a corkscrew?"

"Sounds problematic."

"I think we should keep a low profile."

"I've seen movies where they break off the bottle at the neck."

"In that scenario, are we fishing shards of glass out of our wine?"

"Maybe there's a strainer?"

"Not doing that."

"Right."

We stared at the bottle for a while waiting for an insight. I was beginning to notice something odd about the apartment, something in the back of my mind, it was a sound – a buzzing - but I wasn't concentrating on it since I had a genuine calamity on my hands – wine bottle – no corkscrew.

I asked, "Do you think there's something oddly prophetic about the fact that we can't get the cork out of a bottle from Cork?"

"Cute," Nancy said. But she didn't mean it because

her entire focus was now on getting that wine open. "If we take another knife and start gouging out the cork little by little eventually we will be able to get it out of there without breaking the bottle and we can use the strainer to remove any cork that lands in the wine."

"Why not? We've got time."

I don't want to speculate on how long it took us to gouge out that entire cork from the bottle. It was a tribute to how desperate we were. Suffice to say, dinner was late and you should not try this at home. We agreed though that the wine tasted unusually good after the effort.

We opened the boxes of tepid food and sat down to enjoy our meal. That was when it happened. The buzzing I had heard earlier that I thought must be the old refrigerator – no – FLIES. Everywhere. All at once. We are not talking a fly here or there. We're talking 40 maybe 50 of them excited to ecstasy by the smell of our Chinese food. Which was a double-edged sword based on what a fly's usual diet is we felt the fact that they were attracted to our dinner was distressing.

"What the hell is going on?"

"I hate flies," I practically yelled. "Where did they all come from?"

"Must have gotten trapped in the apartment somehow."

"We have to kill them."

"Or some of them."

"Nancy, I cannot have flies. If there's a bee in my house I have no problem, but flies are disgusting. They're the filthiest insects on the planet. They land their rancid little feet on your food or on your face. No way."

We began Fly-mageddon. With one hand on our wine glasses, we chased and stalked the little suckers all around the living room, balancing on armchairs, standing on the table, killing as many as we could and they just kept coming.

"Here's a little mom tip," I said as I whipped the towel and killed one on the lampshade. "When Olivia was six years old she backed into a Shell No Pest Strip. (SMACK – got another one.) She had really long hair and the strip was basically glued into her hair with a hundred dead bugs."

"Oh, no!" Nancy said. (SMACK)

"She was screaming, 'Get it out – get it out!' Poor little girl was shaking and crying."

"And who can blame her?"

"It looked like I would have to cut the whole thing out, which would have been awful for her because it was all the way up against her scalp. I tried to calm her down as I dialed the company phone number listed on the strip, which I could just make out through her hair. Know what they said?" (SMACK)

"Good one." (SMACK) "What did they say?"

"Peanut butter." (SMACK, SMACK....ugh, smack)

"What?" Nancy landed a very nice strike on a pair of flies cavorting on the sofa.

"Nice hit. Peanut butter. They told me to use peanut butter to get it out of her hair. And what mom doesn't have a handy jar of peanut butter? I massaged it in all around her hair and it worked. The strip slid out."

"Cool."

"Then we shampooed about 15 times and she still smelled like peanut butter for a week. She was really popular with the neighborhood dogs."

It must have taken an hour to get most of the flies and by then we'd finished the wine and we were sloshed. We needed food. We opened back up the Chinese food containers. We ate our cold Chinese food and decided to turn in to our respective bedrooms where we could each read our books and relax in a little unanticipated privacy.

Yeah? No. No privacy. The bedrooms were full of... FLIES. More flies than I had ever seen. First we attacked the ones in Nancy's bedroom. Then we started on the ones in mine.

"You know we might just open the window and try to shoo them out there's so many of them." I crossed to the window. Opened the drapes to find a sign (of course – oh, Ireland) on the window. I read aloud, "'Do NOT open window. It will let in the flies'. Oh my god, are there more out there? I thought every fly in Ireland was in here."

Nancy sighed and closed the drapes. "I can't believe no one checked these rooms before we got here. Obviously, they know there's a problem. Look, there's a sign on every single one of these windows."

"Do you think it's from those lambs we saw outside?"

"Could be."

"They're so cute."

"I think lamb is on the menu."

"Nancy."

"Kidding – but maybe not."

"Well, I can't sleep in here if there are flies. They'll land on my face. They'll buzz all night long."

"Deborah, pretend you're camping."

"I don't camp. I don't tent, or sleep in a bag, or eat trail mix. I don't even understand why anyone does that. I went camping one time. We left our comfortable warm home and set-up camp with another family. Just in case shopping, storing, and feeding your family wasn't enough work, how about you do it without a refrigerator, carrying everything in on your back, cooking on a fire where you can't control the temperature, while standing in dirt, without a sink to wash off anything, and having to trek a distance to a questionably clean stream to wash out your plates, while keeping an eye out for coyotes and bears, only to turn around and carry everything, including your garbage, back out? Camping, I ask you, why? There's a reason Homo Sapiens moved into houses, designed plumbing, installed screens."

When I was done, Nancy smiled tolerantly at me. "Sleep with your head under the covers."

"Okay."

I checked the bed thoroughly and found it insect free. I crawled completely under the covers and tucked it in around me. Lying there scrunched up on my side, deep in a cocoon of bed covers, in the absolute dark, I was completely alone for the first time in a really long time. The emotional and practical chaos of those last weeks while my littlest girl packed up, then the rush to Ireland, the ensuing days full of exciting unpredictable times with my sister, had not allowed for a single moment alone. I supposed that was the point of it all. In a few weeks so much had happened that I hadn't had time to process it all, to mull it over, to think it to death, as my mother used to say. Underneath the covers, lying on my side, all scrunched up, I felt exactly like the little girl in my upstairs bedroom in New Jersey. I used to scrunch up under the covers like that all the time; I felt safe and comforted by the dark and the softness. I don't think I'd done that since those days. As a mom one ear was always outside the covers listening for the baby's cry, and then years later for the car safely in the driveway. Alone in the Ballyknocken House bedroom I remembered being that little girl, lying in my childhood bed, wondering what my life would be. I always knew I would have children – it was only a question of how many. I would have children, raise them, they would grow up, end of story. As a child, I used to listen over and over to Art Gilmore on the record player reading the story of *Diana and the Golden Apples*. It was about a young brave girl who accomplished amazing things and then got married and the story was over. I reviewed in my mind all of the stories and fairytales I knew and realized that they all ended there. The girl gets married — story over. But it doesn't end there. I'm going to make sure my two girls understand that the story doesn't end there. They must think out beyond the family years because there is more, more to plan for, more surprising possibilities for their story, but they must imagine it and plan for that, too. The best lived lives are imagined. I pulled the covers in tightly around me and I felt very alone – a little sad, even lonely, and then Nancy screamed at the top of her lungs and I smiled. I am not alone.

The cooking workshop began at 9:00 a.m. and Nancy knocked on my door around 8:00. "Are you up?"
"Still."
"There's breakfast in the dining room."
"Good. I'll jump in the shower – ready in 10 minutes."
Falling hot water – showers are the most restorative invention of mankind, especially if you've had a rough night's sleep. It is the civilizing element in my day. The shower stall was a cramped space outfitted with a shower curtain that kept getting sucked in and sticking to me, but it felt glorious nonetheless and then cold. AH. No warning, ice cold. I jumped out of the enclosure, grabbed the towel, remembered I had used that towel to kill flies the night before and dropped it immediately disgusted. I stood naked and dripping and freezing. Guess I'll air dry.

There was a pleasant little breakfast prepared in the

dining room with biscuits, jam, quiche, and thankfully coffee. I asked a few times to speak with someone about our rooms, but the girl who was serving breakfast said no one was available since they were prepping for the cooking class. Perhaps after the workshop would be better. I didn't want to ride her since she looked as though serving us had pushed her to the edge of her abilities. We decided to wait.

The classroom was a large rectangular space. The walls were painted red, which I found off-putting. I like red, but I like it in my stoplights and fire trucks. Generally I prefer cool, relaxing colors. Nancy told me I was being contrary. I'm sure she was right.

A demonstration table was set up width-wise in the front of the room. It was equipped with various bowls, spices, and several products that looked very professional. Facing the demonstration table, down the length of the room were six long stainless steel working tables. Each working station had between four and five participants. Nancy and I were standing at a table with two women and one man who looked maybe ten years older than us. We were instructed to put on the chef hats and aprons, which felt a bit gimmicky to me, but I'd had little sleep and a cold shower so I was following Nancy's lead. She actually looked so damn cute in that hat – I looked like a dull-eyed sleepy middle-aged woman with a mushroom cloud blowing out of her head.

The Chef entered. One thing we could say immediately was that Catherine Fulvio was beautiful. She had a charismatic smile and an effervescent personality. I could easily see her on television. Most of the men in the room went goofy.

She introduced the menu: macadamia nut crusted fish, pork tenderloin with an orange marsala sauce, turnips au gratin, Cantonese style roast duck, stir fry vegetables, wasabi mashed potatoes, pesto spiral scones.

She explained, "Different tables are assigned different menu items. When we're all done it will come together and you will enjoy the fabulous meal you made for lunch in our dining room." (Muffled sounds of approval and excitement.) "I will hand out the recipes, divide the meals up between you. I will be here to work with you, show you some tips, and answer all the questions. While I walk around please introduce yourselves to your table mates."

"Hi, I'm Nancy, and this is my sister, Deborah."

"I'm Jan. I'm here with my husband, Howard, and my friend, Mae."

Howard spoke up with an edge, "Yes, Mae came with us on our vacation."

I said, "Nice to meet you."

Mae spoke to him, "I didn't have to come, Howard. I thought you wanted me."

"I left it up to Jan," Howard said.

Jan said, "You were quite clear you had no objection to Mae coming."

"Well, I don't object. I wouldn't say ob-ject."

"Okay," I interrupted, "So Nancy and I are from California. This is our first time in Ireland."

Mae said, "You'll just love it here. The people are so friendly."

Nancy threw me a look. The kitchen helper loaded some ingredients onto our work station and said, "Chef Fulvio will be right over."

I whispered, "Nance, is it me or is there something vaguely sexual about her name, Fulvio?"

"Deborah, get your head in the game, this is varsity cooking."

"I'm just saying."

Chef Fulvio joined us. "Your table will be making the

macadamia nut crusted fish, wasabi mashed potatoes. Here are my recipes."

Mae grabbed the pages. "Great!" She turned to us and said in one breath - "you know I've done such a great deal of cooking and cooking is something I've always been naturally good at, a natural my mother used to say, and when I was little my mother used to let me handle the hot pots even when they were hot because I had a knack, she used to say I had a knack for it, which I always did, it comes from her side of the family, which is the Foster side of the family, and not the Bryne side of the family because oh, no, those folks cannot cook..."

"May I see that?" I interrupted, took the recipe pages, and caught a long-suffering glance from Howard that I now understood. I handed the pages to Nancy.

"Thank you," Nancy said. "So, let's see. First we need 28 grams of butter. Uh, oh."

And that was when it dawned on us.

I turned to Jan and said, "We don't speak metric. I have no idea what a gram is. Is it a teaspoon?"

"We'll do the measuring then. Howard, can you grab that scale and the measuring cups?"

He reached. Mae out-reached him.

"I've got it," Mae said with the kind of excessive cheer that can only come from Prozac. "And these are really good measurers. I like Kitchen Craft. You always know you are getting, what you need. They make every tool it seems for the serious cook and I know a lot of people prefer the Le Creuset but I disagree whole-heartedly and I've had years of experience and..."

Nancy had her head down and may have been laughing. She had more patience than me because I didn't sleep due to the buzzing and was still not over the cold shower and naked drip-dry experience from earlier.

"Mae," I interrupted.

"Yes?"

"Could you pass that bag of macadamia nuts?"

"Oh, sure, sure, I'm a big nut person you know nutritionally speaking they have everything you could..."

"Here, Howard." I handed him the pounder. "Why don't you pound down those nuts."

He smiled, grabbed the pounder, and began with gusto. This was a guy who clearly needed to hit something.

Chef Fulvio asked, "Who would like to go out to the Herb Garden with me and pick some..."

"Mae," I yelled. "Mae wants to go. Don't you, Mae?"

"Surely I do. I know so much about herbs. I've always had a really successful herb garden of my own and as I recall one season I had a prize winning rosemary bush that I..."

And she was gone. I heard Howard exhale. He looked up for a moment with a grateful half-smile at me and then went back to pounding.

Nancy turned to Jan. "Dividing up the work then. Why don't you prep the fish? Deborah and I will begin peeling the potatoes for the wasabi mashed."

"Wow," I said. "That's a lot of potatoes."

"There are about 20 of us."

"Isn't there someone whose job it is to peel for us? I would think for this price there'd be a peeling person assigned to each table."

"Stop," Nancy handed me the peeler. "Go."

And that's pretty much how it went. The chef talked, worked on some peaches for dessert, called some of the guys up to the demonstration table where she flirted with them, which they loved. I volunteered Mae for everything, and then I sent her to "help" people at other tables. This did not make me popular, but Howard had pulverized the macadamia nuts and still wouldn't let go of the pounder, so I had some valid concerns.

"Nancy? What's the look for?"

"This recipe doesn't seem right."

"In what way?"

"I've made an awful lot of mashed potatoes in my life – and while I've not done the wasabi, I don't think there's enough salt or sour cream or anything else actually in this recipe. It'll be dry, tasteless."

"She is the chef. Let's follow the recipe and see what comes out."

"I guess."

Chef Fulvio checked with us regularly. She was very charming. Nancy may have mentioned that the recipe looked a little light on some of the needed ingredients, at which point she gave us a brilliantly white smile, which definitely came from a bleaching gel, and moved on.

Three hours later, the entire meal was done. We were to leave our results and walk over to the dining room where we would be served and have a chance to taste everything on the menu. As people were taking off their aprons...

Nancy tested the mashed potatoes. "Cardboard."

The chef came over, "How are they?"

"It needs more salt, maybe a little skim milk to lighten it up a bit without adding more fat, and then much more wasabi."

"Oh." The chef looked perplexed. "Well, whatever you think." She gave us another perky smile and she walked away.

"Whatever I think?" Nancy turned to me, "I think this tastes like wallpaper paste."

Howard tasted it and nodded. "Discount wallpaper paste".

"Can you fix it?" Jan asked Nancy.

"I think so."

"Go for it." And then I whispered in her ear. "But hurry. I want to make sure we aren't sitting at lunch next to Mae."

"Good thinking." Nancy went to work. She threw aside the recipe and started adding things in a whirlwind of raw instinct. She didn't measure, she didn't consider, she moved with confidence, and in one minute she turned those wallpaper paste potatoes into something silky, yummy, with just the right bite of wasabi – delicious.

Jan and Howard tasted. They grinned.

I considered the recipe again. "Did we do something wrong?"

Jan answered. "We followed the directions exactly."

"Interesting."

On our way to the dining room, Nancy and I darted ahead of Jan, Howard, and Mae and we joined a couple who looked in their 20s already seated at a table for four. (I felt I'd done what I could for poor Howard and he was on his own.) Each table got a sampling of each of the items the group had prepared. I don't eat pork or duck so I put the fish on my plate along with the potatoes and a scone. I was happy with that. Nancy, Mike and Gwen passed the plates taking a little of everything.

"Oh, you're newlyweds?" Nancy handed Gwen the pork. "So great. Seems like a long time since we got married, doesn't it, Deborah?"

"It was a long time, over 20 years."

Mike said gently, "Oh, are your husbands dead?"

I looked up from my plate startled. "Dead? No."

"You're traveling without your husbands on purpose?" Mike asked nonplussed.

"Boy, you are young," I said.

"Deborah," Nancy chided me and then turned to Mike. "Yes, we are on a sister trip together."

Mike looked confused, "Uh, huh."

Gwen was a small, thin, precocious dark-haired girl who reminded us both of our sister Eileen, so we liked her instantly. He was a burly outdoorsy type. They were really cute together.

"Well," Gwen explained, "we were *supposed* to live in Dublin the first two years."

"We loved Dublin," Nancy said.

"That was the plan," Gwen said and rolled her eyes.

Mike shrugged. "A plan is just a plan. It's not a thing – it's a plan."

I was curious. "You are not going to Dublin then?"

"You see, the *plan* was Mike and I were going to take over his dad's farm when he retired in a few years. Meanwhile, the farmhouse needed renovations and so we were going to live in Dublin and love the city life, the restaurants, and fun things to do, while we renovated the farmhouse. After that we were going to move in, after two years or so. That *was* the plan."

Nancy took a bite of the pork. "It's no longer the plan?"

Gwen looked at Mike and he explained, "My dad got high blood pressure and he had to stop working so now instead we are going directly to take over the farm."

"Which was *not* the plan," Gwen added.

Mike shrugged.

"The farm," Gwen went on, "is in the middle of nowhere. I mean nowhere. There's no town nearby and no neighbors in sight and I don't know anyone anyway. I figured we would renovate, enjoy living in Dublin for a couple of years, and then when we were ready to have children we would move out to the farm. That was the plan."

"I see," Nancy said.

"So instead, now, I will be stuck in a house while it's being rebuilt in the middle of nowhere, with no friends, no children, and a husband working sun-up to sun-down. I'm just making the point that it was not..."

I finished her sentence, "the plan.'

"Precisely."

"Has anyone tried the pork?" Nancy asked. "I can't even chew it."

Mike answered, "Like tire tread."

"Well, the fish is dry as sand and I actually think I chipped a tooth on that pesto scone," I admitted.

Nancy put down her fork. "Don't bother eating the duck, it's all sauce."

"Do we have any left-over Chinese food in the fridge?" I asked.

Mike perked up. "You have a stash of Chinese food?'

"No, we got rid of it all last night."

"Do you think this whole meal is our fault? We made it," I asked.

"We followed the recipes," Gwen said. "A recipe is like a plan and one should follow it."

"Maybe at dinner tonight when *they* do the cooking it will be better?" Mike tried to be positive.

We saw no point in pretending to eat and so we wished the newlyweds luck and headed back toward our apartment.

Nancy was grinning. "I think Mike's in for a rough road."

"Agreed. I felt sorry for Gwen though. It would be miserable to be stuck out in the middle of nowhere like that."

"Which was clearly not..."

Together, "the *plan*."

"Nancy, the only edible item on that menu were the

potatoes you doctored at the last minute."

"I did expect more. I'm disappointed."

We opened the door to the apartment and FLIES! All over. The housekeeper, who must have been illiterate and so couldn't read the signs posted *on every single window* had opened every single window. The apartment sounded like a lawn mower.

"Nancy, I know Ballyknocken was your thing, the cooking school, and being here but..."

"Yeah, this is bad."

"We're booked for another night." I looked around at the swarming black menace. "I'd rather not do this again with the flies, and I'm not exactly looking forward to her dinner either if lunch was any preview."

"Want to go?"

"I could stay, if we change rooms. This is your call though." I wanted to be sure. This cooking school had been Nancy's one non-negotiable, in the same way that the Abbeyglen-not-a-castle Castle had been mine. How interesting it was that both our must-see situations were not what we expected, but they were still the stories we were sure we'd tell over and over. "We can go see if they have a different room. What do you want?"

"I want to run away from here as fast as we can."

"We'll lose that money."

"I don't care."

"Me, either."

"Let's go. We will stop at Glendalough to see the ruins, and then keep going all the way to Dublin and spend the extra night there before we head home."

Here we were sneaking around again. We felt embarrassed to leave so noticeably. To say to this place we would rather pay and leave than pay and stay. Everyone had been very nice and we knew it would be painfully awkward if we saw the Chef or anyone else while we were running away. We threw our stuff in the suitcase (dodging flies), closed the door, rolled to the car, and quickly loaded our things.

"We have to check out," Nancy said. "Or they'll expect us for dinner. And they were going to run our credit card for the rooms, we've already paid for the workshop."

"Okay, let's hurry."

We entered the little foyer and found the girl who had been serving breakfast. We were relieved – at first.

"Your information will be on the computer," she said.

"Okay," Nancy responded. "So, pull it up."

"The computer isn't on."

Nancy kindly said, "Can you please turn it on?"

"I can't."

"You aren't allowed?"

"I don't know how."

Nancy and I looked at each other. Nancy tried again, "You mean you don't know how to search for the right file?"

She looked at us very blankly, "No, I don't know how to turn it on at all."

I had to jump in here just to be sure I understood. "You're saying you don't know how to switch on a computer?"

"I don't."

"Would you like us to turn it on for you?" Nancy asked.

"Oh, no. No one is allowed to touch the computer."

"I see," said Nancy with her enviable patience. "How about you just run our credit card for what we owe and you can make the computer changes later when the office person returns."

"I don't know how."

Poor girl, I thought, she looked so lost and worried.

The girl continued, "But I'm *sure* you're staying to-night. It says so right here in the book."

We made every human attempt to explain to her that regardless of what she thought, or what she was told, or what she was reading in the book, we were leaving. When five minutes stretched into twenty minutes as she wandered around aimlessly trying to figure out what to do, we became increasingly uncomfortable thinking the Chef or another guest might come upon us and we would have to explain why we were leaving and we simply didn't want to have that conversation. We left all of our credit card information with the bewildered girl, told her to just charge it when she figured out how, and send a receipt. We trusted her because she was clearly incapable of doing anything nefarious...well...anything at all. We bolted to the car and honestly felt like we were on the run. Weeks later we received in the mail a receipt from Ballyknocken House where it showed they did not charge us for that second night, which was incredibly thoughtful, especially since they had no idea why we'd left. Perhaps someone had gone to check on our rooms and had been carried away by flies, and so they divined the problem. In any event, we had intended to pay and they didn't charge us – nice. Now, all they needed to do was kill the flies, and, oh yeah, learn to cook.

For the first time since we lifted-off from home the end of our trip was in sight. We had one more stop: Glendalough. After that we would continue on to Dublin for our last night in Ireland. I didn't know at this moment as I drove toward Glendalough how very different-ly Nancy and I were seeing our approach home. I was to learn that later in Dublin.

HALLELUJAH

Glendalough is a monastic ruin, south of Dublin, in Wicklow National Park. It was high up on my Most Wanted list. The monastery was founded by (Coemgen) Kevin, now St. Kevin. Kevin was ordained into the Catholic Church and set off to live a hermitic ascetic life. The legend is that he lived alone in the wild, sleeping in a tiny rock cave for many years, and slowly followers gathered around him and a monastery grew up – this was Glendalough and for a long time it was a significant spiritual center.

Sources claim Kevin was born in 498, which puts him just a little later in time than St. Patrick. The reason I said "claimed" was because all those same sources put his death in June 618, thereby making him 120 years old. 120? Come on. And the sources state this fact as though it's the most natural thing in the world – with no comment. With state-of-the-art 21st century medicine, antibiotics, sterile surgery units, machines that can breathe for you, and pump your heart, and evacuate your bowels, we *still* can't live to 120. What was that other guy's name again – Doubting Thomas? And, I ask you: who would want to live to 120 years old? Shall we do a middle-age inventory? Already my hair is graying, my skin is dry, I need reading glasses, and I can't hear in a crowded room, and I'm not even half that age yet. And the ascetics were especially known for dying young due to the stress on their bodies. Francis of Assisi was only 44 years old when he died. I suppose it was the authority with which all of the sources simply stated, oh, yeah, he was 120 years old that miffed me.

What appealed to me about Kevin were the folktales that have endured about his life. He has been the inspiration for songs, for films, for a series of paintings by Clive Hicks-Jenkins and a famous poem by the Nobel Laureate Seamus Heaney. The poem *St Kevin and the Blackbird* references this story: One day, Kevin was kneeling stationary in prayer with his arms extended palms up for such a long time that a blackbird nested in his palm. Feeling his oneness with nature and "the network of eternal life", Kevin remained motionless until the eggs hatched.

A lovely and inspirational story about patience and the connection to nature; but, then, there was another story. A young beautiful woman named Kathleen fell hard for the handsome reclusive young priest. It was said she pursued him aggressively and Kevin in a fit of pique for being tempted threw her off the cliff and into the water where she drowned. Some researchers and writers argue this is not true and they defend Kevin by saying he did not throw her into the lake, he only beat her with nettles. This evidently did not interfere with his road to canonization.

We arrived and parked. This was the only place we visited our entire time in Ireland where a sign (yes, a sign) told us not to leave our valuables in the car. Surprising, and also, disappointing. The most spiritual place? Where monks eschewed worldly possessions?

Nancy and I noted the irony, locked our car door, and proceeded onto the property.

Glendalough far exceeded our expectations. A large complex with many ancient stone structures in various states, and much better preserved than we'd expected. You could spend most of the day just trying to make-out the words chiseled into the ancient tombstones. This place got under our skin. We didn't talk much. We just wandered around alone together musing about the world these people knew and how long ago they lived their lives here, how they worried and fought and cried and made plans as though each thing mattered, and then how monumentally insignificant it all turned out to be. May be a good lesson in keeping perspective.

In the middle of the cemetery was the largest ruin called the Cathedral, whose walls were over three feet thick and where you could stand in the middle and see exactly what they saw when looking out centuries ago. To the south of the Cathedral was St. Kevin's Cross, over 11 feet tall, and presumably where Kevin is buried (at 120 years old). There was a classic, intact, Irish Round Tower, 110 feet high, which we could not enter (probably a good thing based on our last tower excursion). The date of construction is not known but the speculation is 6th century. This place was astonishing and mystical.

There were bucolic paths through the woods that led to the lakes, and to many other sights, well worth the hike. Once we got a little look around we were not surprised that so many tourists came here, or that there were numerous school children racing in and out and up and down and yelling and challenging each other and totally missing the history all around them.

Field trips are wasted on the young. How great would it be if someone knocked on your door and took you on a field trip to a museum or some great historical place where they'd arranged for a guide and tickets for you and you brought a sack lunch of peanut butter and jelly with an apple? How great? You didn't have to find the place, buy the tickets, hire a guide, make the snack, or arrange for transportation. Nice. Again, wasted on the kids. Maybe there's a business here: AFT, Inc. Adult Field Trips. Each city could have a chapter and arrange day trips for the local adults who'd thoroughly appreciate it.

I did volunteer for most of the school field trips when my kids were little. I didn't do anything else at the school, unlike Nancy who managed everything and really deserved a salary, but if they were throwing the kids en masse into a bus and taking them off school grounds I was in. It wasn't completely that I didn't trust the chaperones; it was just slightly that I didn't trust the chaperones. I would have been okay with most of the teachers, but sometimes a coach would fill in. I have a particular antipathy and distrust for school coaches. And not solely because the coach at our high school was playing boys on the baseball team based on which mom he was sleeping with, or because another coach threatened to throw my kid off the team because I said she wouldn't play with 103 fever and strep throat, or because a coach at Nancy's school was convicted of stealing the booster club money. Nope, my antipathy started way before high school. In my experience, if you want to find an under-qualified, narcissistic, megalomaniacal, power hungry nitwit, just take a gander at children's sports. Moms out there know exactly who I'm talking about. That bloated my-glory-days-were-in-middle-school coach who held your child's self-esteem in the palm of his hand, never played fair, and believed that his little fiefdom was more important than schoolwork or health concerns. You know, the guy who ran your kid around the field 18 times in one hundred degree heat to make a point about who was boss, in case your nine-year-old didn't know. Really? Were the dance and volleyball coaches hired because they lacked any semblance of a rational perspective or appropriate temperament? And did it *specify* humorless in the job qualifications? I don't know a single mother who hasn't wanted to smack a coach at one time or another. So many coach horror stories, and so many times when they could have been human – but weren't. Perhaps I'm painting with too broad of a brush; perhaps there are some really wonderful coaches. I'll stipulate to that. We just never had one. Our first experience set the standard for every one that followed.

It was the first little league T-ball practice game of the season. The boys were five years old. Jeff was put at second base. Like the other kids this was his first game and he was five, so the rules were a bit fuzzy, and all he absolutely understood was that it was his job not to let the runner get to second base. The at-bat kid hit the ball off the T-bar and it sputtered down the field. The runner, already at first base, took off toward the second base and Jeff. Jeff was committed. He is just the kind of kid who is *all in – always.* As the little runner approached him, with no ball in sight, Jeff did the only thing he could think to do. He picked up second base and started running away with it. The runner pursued. Jeff ran around the field with the base runner chasing him trying to touch the base. The parents in the stands were doubled-over laughing. Both these little boys were desperately committed and running around as fast as they could. Jeff would turn right, deek left, the kid would mimic and they'd be off again. There wasn't a mom or dad in the bleachers who wasn't hysterical. When the two little boys finally stopped from exhaustion, and the parents sides hurt from laughing, instead of calmly instructing these two five-year-old boys, who had clearly given it *everything they had*, the red-faced, eye-bulging, angry – yes, angry – coach screamed at both boys until they started crying. The parents were stunned to silence.

Sure, there may be a good coach or two out there, but on average, it was *that* guy. And then, right there, in the spiritual cathedral at Glendalough, Nancy and I had an epiphany! A genuine enlightening and blissful insight – we would never...ever... have to mollify, manipulate, placate, or genuflect, to another school coach – ever again. Hallelujah! RIP.

BACK TO DUBLIN

Did we know we should go to a budget hotel for our last night in Dublin? Of course we did. Did we have a reservation at a budget hotel in Dublin for our last night? Of course we did. Did we go back to the Shelbourne for our last night? Of course we did.

"Sisters. Welcome back," Keith said as we passed the concierge desk.

"Hi, Keith. Hey, we need to return the rental car what is the best way to do that?"

"I'll do that for you."

"Really?"

"Sure. Let me give them a call. Where is the car now?"

"Right in front with Jiminey Cricket."

"All right. No problem."

How could you not love Keith? We checked in, took two brownies from the smiling desk girl, asked for a room *not* on the same floor as the crying ghost of little Mary. We walked to the elevator (nicer than my living room), marveled at the spotless hallway, found our room, and both flopped face down on the beds. They were luxuriously soft, smelled fresh, and there was no buzzing. It was heavenly.

"Where should we go for dinner?"

"Wherever Keith says."

"Perfect."

"Then, one more pub."

"O'Donoghues on Baggot Street. We saved it for our last night."

Nancy rolled out of bed and headed for the bathroom. I was feeling sleepy, which was odd for me. I usually have a dip at the end of a day but this was more of a plunge. I had sunk into the bed like I weighed two thousand pounds. I felt I might actually sleep. I was in that alpha land when...

"Ow! Oh, damn! Damn! NO. No."

I was out of bed and running to the bathroom. "What?"

Nancy's face was under the flowing sink faucet and she was blinking her eyes. "I put the wrong drops in my eyes."

"No. What, oh shit. What can I do?"

"I'm flushing. Stings. Stings."

"What did you put in?" I grabbed the bottle. It was contact lens cleaning solution.

"I was trying to put in some saline because they were so dry. I grabbed the wrong bottle."

"Oh, god."

I grabbed the bottle and ran to my computer in the other room to look up the best course of action. We had been too cheap to pay the 20 euro for the Internet for one night so I couldn't connect. I called down to the desk and tried to change that immediately – they were working on it. I searched the tiny print on the bottle for a phone number of the company. No phone number? In the U.S. all products must have a phone number on the label. Someone somewhere passed a law for that, and in a country where I often complain there are way too many laws, I was frustrated to find no phone number on this label right then. This was a European product and I guess they don't do that. I felt like every second mattered and I had no Internet and no phone number for advice. I was missing the U.S.A. right then.

"Nancy, c'mon we need to go to the hospital. Can't waste time."

"Ow. No, I'm flushing."

"We have to see an eye doctor."

"No."

"Nancy, it's your eyes – you don't get another pair."

"I'm doing the right thing."

She was adamant that she was not going anywhere. I ran back to the computer and still couldn't get the Internet up. I felt so helpless.

Nancy said, "Damn TSA."

"Hey, I'm a big fan of blaming things on airport security but how'd they do this?"

"I always have two differently shaped bottles: one saline, and the other cleanser so I don't make this mistake. When I got to security on the way here they wouldn't let me bring the cleanser because it was an ounce over the rules. So I had to leave it and then buy it here that first day, but this is an Irish product and bottles are identical shapes and so I grabbed the wrong one."

Minutes went by and I was amazed at how long Nancy could hold her face under water while the faucet flushed past her eye. Then, she pulled her head out and looked in the mirror. The whites of her left eye were bright red.

"Nancy."

"It's stopped stinging. I think it's going to okay."

"You think...you think."

"Deborah, I know you have never worn contacts, but I've had them my whole life and what I need to do is keep flushing and not go running around looking for a doctor to tell me to keep flushing."

Nancy could be beautifully reasonable. I was not happy, but I bowed to her experience. It was very stressful for me because I felt the whole time like we should be doing something more proactive. Slowly over the course of the evening she turned out to be right as her eye healed.

What was notable about this episode was it slapped us back to reality. We had had no cares and had been floating along in this foreign world. This moment reminded us, signaled to us, that our sojourn was over. Reality — and everything that went with it — came roaring back. I wasn't sure I was ready for that.

Since it was our last night we decided to take a long walk to Temple Bar for dinner. We had a reservation at La Caverna on Fownes Street. We split a salad and then split an entrée – we felt it was appropriate to get half a dinner since they had seated us at half a table. This tiny table for two was pushed against a modern-esque stone wall and very near a staircase. Wait staff and customers walked by us in a constant flow and I found I couldn't move my right arm without hitting the wall. I know we've established I'm not a foodie, but I do enjoy being able to use both hands while eating.

After dinner, we trekked over to O'Donoghues Pub on Baggot Street. The building dates from 1789 and became a pub in 1934. Pub is short for public house and this was a public house on steroids. It was jammed in a way that is challenging to describe. Evening pub-goers were shoulder-to-shoulder, stomach-to-side, and back-to-back, from the far end corner of the bar to people spilling out all over the street. Gaggles of Dubliners were having their entire nightly pub experience on the sidewalk in front because they couldn't get inside.

No maximum occupancy laws here. I wasn't completely convinced there was enough oxygen in there. This, however, was our last night and we were not to be thwarted. I dropped my head and ploughed into the crowd hoping I looked a bit desperate and on my way to the bathroom or somewhere specific. Nancy grabbed my arm and followed. I knew the mistake was to slow down or stop. As long as we kept pushing, literally pushing, through and repeating "excuse me" we would make progress. All the way into the very back corner of the bar we found a two-foot space where we could wedge ourselves. We had come to O'Donoghues to hear the traditional music, for which the pub was famous, and which we had been told numerous times was an indispensable cultural element of Ireland. We had heard it here and there as we had traveled around but hadn't spent any time listening. (Another acquired mommy talent: hearing without listening.) Tonight was our last opportunity to enjoy the trad music. We listened as they played and soon understood that the tedious repetitiveness of this music explained why everyone drinks. Holy shit, get me a couple of shots.

Practically standing on top of me Nancy still had to yell to be heard. "I guess it has to grow on you."

"Well, it's better than bagpipes," I yelled back.

"Marginally."

"How long do you think before we will get a drink in here?"

"Six, seven months."

"We def cannot stay here sober."

"Agreed."

"So, you feel you've enjoyed this cultural experience then?"

"I have."

I put down my head and we ploughed our way right

out of there.

We walked slowly back to the Shelbourne where we took a comfortable seat in the No. 27 bar and had come full circle. We ordered the same two drinks we had the day we arrived when we were jet-lagged and sad. We sat for a long time silently lost in our own thoughts.

"Nancy, I dread going home." I felt teary.

"You do?" She was visibly surprised.

"Yeah."

"I'm ready. I want to see Chip, and be in the same time zone as my kids, hug my dog, and when I see Hobie do you know what I'm going to do?"

"What?"

"I'm going to give him two bowls of food. What the hell, he's 12 years old, he can't see, he can barely hear, and all he wants in the world is two bowls of food."

"I like it." I lifted my glass, "Here's to livin' large." I downed my cocktail.

"Okay, Deborah, what's wrong?"

"All good."

"C'mon."

"I don't know exactly. I do know that I liked the constant challenge and chaos of raising kids. It isn't only their presence that I'll miss, but the drama of it all was invigorating. I prefer unpredictability. I dread the empty routine waiting for me back home. I don't want to stroll calmly into the sunset with fat kneecaps. I don't want Calming Ahead."

"What do you want?"

"I want to approach the sunset on a dead run, slightly off-balance, with my shoes untied."

"Does sound like you."

We ordered our second and our last drink in Ireland. I asked my little sister, "Do you feel differently from when you arrived? Do you think this trip was good for you?"

"Yes. Being away from home and experiencing all new things, somewhere along the way my perspective shifted. It was like I put on a panoramic lens. My life looks more like a play to me now. I recognize that being a career mom was an act in the play of my life, and it may be the best act in my life, but I can't really know that yet, can I? I'm never going to stop missing having my kids living at home, but where we are in life right now, is also temporary," Nancy said thoughtfully. "It's temporary."

"How so?"

Nancy put down her drink and looked at me for a moment. When she spoke again there was a wistful seriousness to her tone.

"Deborah, we don't know what's ahead. The idea that tomorrow is a given and will be much like today is a fantasy."

"But that's how people live, with that expectation."

"I've seen my friends' lives change in an instant from an unexpected circumstance both good and bad."

"We've seen that in our own family a few times."

"We don't know what our health may be in a week, or what our finances might be in a month from now. We don't know in what way we may be wanted or needed by our children, our parents, our husbands, our grandchildren, or each other. The only thing I'm sure of is we *will* be needed in some way at some point. I know that in my gut. We are more free at this one moment in time than we have ever been, or may ever be, in our entire lives."

"That's true."

"This freedom may end next week, or it may last a year, a couple of years, we simply can't predict it. There's your unpredictability."

"I suppose."

"And when that moment comes that we're needed by our family or our friends, for any reason, for illness, or grandchildren, or job loss, or celebrations, whatever, we'll be there, because we will want to be there, because it is our nature to be there."

"It is our nature."

"Yes."

"But it isn't *all* we are."

"No, it isn't," Nancy reasoned. "And that's my point. We saw our kids leaving home as an end, which it was, and it hurt, still does. But I've realized on this trip that for us this is really just an intermission. The intermission in our play. A huge unanticipated gift." Nancy sipped her drink. "And I've always really liked intermission: you get to stretch, have a snack, share a few thoughts about the preceding act, and a few laughs about the performance of others. If we hadn't taken this trip I don't think I would have thought about where we are right now in quite that way."

"Well, if this is my intermission, then I want to make theatrical choices."

"You want to plan for another trip?" Nancy said and I nodded. She continued, "I've kind of always wanted to go to the Netherlands."

"Did you know at the Hotel De Vrouwe van Stavoren we can sleep inside a 14,500 litre Swiss wine barrel?"

"Uh, Deborah, I like the wine idea, but only if I'm drinking it."

"It's supposed to be quite comfortable."

"I'll think about that. What about Finland?"

"Yes. At the Hotel Kakslauttanen we can stay inside a glass igloo."

"You want to sleep in an igloo? I can't imagine what

the bedding is like in an igloo. You think I'm screaming now?"

"It's warm even though it's 250 miles inside the Arctic Circle. At night, when you lie in your bed, it's nothing but stars."

"I was considering something more civilized and a lot warmer."

"Okay. In Provence, there's a Bed & Breakfast called The Orion that is an actual tree house."

"A tree house sounds better than the Arctic Circle. But since we're unsure how long this intermission might last we need to think about cost," Nancy warned.

"That's an issue. Maybe we should consider a trip closer to home?"

"We could drive across the country. Another road trip but this time on the right side of the road? There's so much of North America I haven't seen."

"Two Broads and a mini-van?"

"Why not? There are music festivals, foodie festivals, Earth and nature festivals, beer festivals, even chocolate festivals."

"There are alternative festivals, too, like the Roswell UFO festival and Burning Man."

"It's intermission. So, let's stretch."

When we were three little girls growing up together in a tiny wooded New Jersey town our parents used to tell us that in life you only needed three things to be happy: someone to love, someone who loved you, and something to look forward to. We loved our families – they loved us – and we went to sleep our last night in Ireland dreaming of new places to look forward to. It was our intermission and we planned to eat, drink, stretch our world and enjoy it for however long it lasted.

EPILOGUE

The 2010 U.S. census listed five million women who identified themselves as stay-at-home mothers, whose full-time occupation was caring for their children. Statistics from the National Center for Education indicated that every year more than three million high school seniors graduate and move on with their own lives. That's a lot of moms left behind.

Every mother who has watched a child pack up and move out has experienced some feelings of loss, or at the very least a fundamental alteration in their daily workload. The transition to an empty nest elicits a great deal of emotion – some of this emotion women try to hide, because they feel slightly embarrassed, or a little silly. Instead of watching your world shrink take a trip, grab a friend and go somewhere you've never been. It doesn't have to be an exotic trip; it can be a drive, just far enough away for a long enough time that it allows you to leave the loss behind and feel the freedom ahead.

There has been a proliferation of websites, books, and travel agencies targeting women. Travel is at the top of the list of many women in their 50s looking for an adventure and needing to see their lives from a different angle. Run away from home, alone, with a sister, with a girlfriend – look forward to it.

Adventure Women
www.adventurewomen.com

Adventures For Women
www.adventuresforwomen.org

Walking Women
www.walkingwomen.com

Sights and Soul Travelers – Tours and Vacations for Women
www.sightsandsoul.com

Wanderlust and Lipstick: Your Destination for Women's Travel
www.wanderlustandlipstick.com

Adventures In Good Company: Adventure Travel For Women of All Ages
www.adventuresingoodcompany.com

Canyon Calling Tours – Multi-Sport Adventures for Women Over 30
www.canyoncalling.com

Journey Women
www.Journeywomen.com

Women Traveling Together
www.women-traveling.com

Made in the USA
Middletown, DE
09 November 2015